Beyond EHR

Using Technology to Meet Growing Demands and Deliver Better Patient Care

Beyond EHR

Using Technology to Meet Growing Demands and Deliver Better Patient Care

Jeffery Daigrepont, EFMP, CAPPM

Foreword by James Morrow, MD, Morrow Family Medicine

CRC Press
Taylor & Francis Group
Boca Raton London New York

CRC Press is an imprint of the
Taylor & Francis Group, an **informa** business

A PRODUCTIVITY PRESS BOOK

First published 2021
by CRC Press
600 Broken Sound Parkway #300, Boca Raton FL, 33487

and by CRC Press
2 Park Square, Milton Park, Abingdon, Oxon, OX14 4RN
CRC Press is an imprint of the Taylor & Francis Group, an informa business

ISBN: 9780367405540 (hbk)
ISBN: 9780367374365 (pbk)
ISBN: 9780429356674 (ebk)

Typeset in Garamond
By Deanta Global Publishing Services, Chennai, India

Contents

Foreword

As an early adopter of electronic medical records (EHR), I have been heavily involved in attaining every benefit possible from the use of technology in my family practice in the northern suburbs of Atlanta, Georgia. I met Jeffery Daigrepont with Coker Group about 20 years ago at a HIT industry trade show. I have crossed paths, attended presentations and interacted with him throughout these years as we participated in various HIMSS and other IT conferences.

The extensive content of this book, coupled with Jeffery's straightforward and down-to-earth style, will inform and assist you with some of the most pertinent, though confusing, aspects of HIT. As physicians move beyond EHRs, it is refreshing to have someone with Jeffery's knowledge and expertise to help guide us through these decisions. One of those issues is the lack of interoperability and how to improve it. It is also helpful to understand how we get data to and from other practices securely to ensure our patient's medical record is complete and current.

Another critical challenge for physicians is how to contract and negotiate with vendors to achieve the best possible arrangements so that we can practice as we want through technology customizations. We are often victims of vendors over-promising and under-delivering. This book will offer many tips and recommendations on how to avoid those pitfalls and protect one of the most significant investments you will make in your career. I would not recommend signing a vendor contract without having someone with Jeffery's objective and unbiased perspective to sort through the unfavorable terms and conditions and to avoid unforeseen expenditures.

Beyond navigating the uncertainties of the HIT market, this book offers guidance on using telemedicine as a delivery model. Although the COVID-19 pandemic "forced" physicians to implement telemedicine, it has turned out well and may be a permanent part of patient encounters in the future.

My practice was ready to provide telemedicine through the technology investments we had made and continue to pursue. Through telemedicine encounters, we were able to deliver ongoing care to our patients when presenting at my office was undesirable. We had open access!

I firmly believe that physicians and healthcare providers who are reluctant to venture into new applications would be more comfortable moving forward in healthcare information technology if they had a broader understanding of its benefits and expectations for the future. Practitioners who read this book will learn how IT will work for them with sound guidance from an experienced and impartial source.

James Morrow, M.D.
Morrow Family Medicine

Dr. James Morrow graduated from Clemson University and the University of South Carolina School of Medicine. He completed his residency in Family Medicine in Anderson, South Carolina, in 1985. A 2004 winner of the Healthcare Information Management Systems Society's (HIMSS) Davies Award for Excellence in EMR Implementation, he was also recognized as the 2006 Physician IT Leader of the Year by HIMSS. Dr. Morrow was named the 2014 Entrepreneur of the Year by the Cumming Forsyth County Chamber of Commerce and the 2014 Community Leader of the Year by the Metro Atlanta Chamber of Commerce. Morrow Family Medicine was named "Best of Forsyth" five years in a row, 2015 through 2019.

Through the Morrow Community Foundation, d.b.a. The Forsyth BYOT Benefit, the Morrows began supporting the technology initiative in the Forsyth County Schools. The charity raises money to provide technology (Internet and devices) to students in the county who do not have them. In seven years, the Foundation has raised over $350,000 so that every student in the county who needs access to technology has it. This access has been incredibly important during the 2020 pandemic.

Preface

Writing a second edition to the *Complete Guide and Toolkit to Successful EHR Adoption*, published in 2011 by HIMSS, would suggest there is still an opportunity to discuss EHR *adoption*. While many of the concepts and strategies offered in the first edition remain valid today, we now have an 87% adoption rate of EHRs nationwide.[1] Nevertheless, many still question the benefits and achievements since 2011, when the Institute of Medicine (IOM), delivered a publication on *Health IT and Patient Safety: Building Safer Systems for Better Care*. This report, chartered by the National Academy of Sciences to advise the federal government on issues of medical care, research and education, called for a national effort to make healthcare safer using electronic health records (EHR). Many providers/hospitals have struggled with EHR adoption or purchased a system that is no longer commercially available. In contrast, others have had success and have achieved positive results in improving outcomes and patient safety.

The HCIT industry has also evolved significantly, most notably through vendor consolidation. The vendor market that once comprised several hundred EHR vendors has now been reduced to a handful over a brief period, with consolidation continuing daily. Concurrently, there has been a significant expansion in innovation and facilitating solutions beyond the core EHR system. Most of this innovation has been to improve the ease of use and the overall performance of EHR systems. For example, interoperability, which is the focus of Chapter 9, continues to be a significant challenge in the adoption/utilization of EHRs. In the early years, EHR systems could not communicate with one another, so despite the attempts at automation, there were few perceived benefits to the consumer or caregiver. Practices were printing summaries of the encounter captured in their EHR and faxing or mailing these documents to other caregivers who would scan (upload) the materials into their EHRs. The information was created electronically, converted to paper, then reconverted electronically as a scanned image. There were also no programming standards or capability standards. Moreover, there were significant concerns within the OIG of EHR systems about producing a *cloned note* and over-enhancing coding/documentation to drive up the level of the visit, delivering higher fees to the government and patients. A cloned note is when an EHR template for documenting a visit is used verbatim for every patient with the same condition. This duplication enables the provider to document the patient record faster. Still, there is an increased risk of unintentional fraud, as it suggests every patient interaction was the same, which would be unlikely. Thus, significant EHR standards and policies were adopted during the Obama administration tied to incentives and penalties to curb abuse on both the provider and vendor side. This initiative later became the Meaningful Use (MU) EHR incentive program. Vendors that demonstrated mandated capabilities received a certification status. Providers who adopted certified EHRs and demonstrated MU with the certified EHR were rewarded with financial incentives. The implementation of the Meaningful Use program was over several phases/years, with each phase building on the previous one. Though the program mostly worked as intended, there was little oversight and/or verification. Qualification primarily relied on an attestation, which is another word for the honor system. Today, vendors and providers are being audited, and many are having to return the money and/or pay major false claims settlement fines to the government.[2] This matter is discussed more in-depth later in this book, but it illustrates nearly a complete reversal, from paying physicians/hospitals to adopt EHRs, to what we now see as efforts to claw back some of this money paid out, which is estimated to be $6 billion.[3]

In closing, it has been extremely gratifying to have published a book on EHR adoption and to have witnessed this adoption come about. The process was long and hard, but it has set up the foundation for going beyond EHRs in a way that will fundamentally change how we deliver and access care in the United States. The innovation we address in this book would not have been possible had it not been for the industry leaders. Associations, such as HIMSS, bring together key stakeholders from all sectors of the industry (policy, providers, technologies, innovators) to inspire and work together on this journey. Additional credit and appreciation go to all the early EHR adopters who put in the time and work, made the sacrifices and never gave up in their quest for a better EHR. There are now generations of HITECH professionals ready to lead us into the future, as we go beyond EHRs, who will hopefully benefit from this book. Enjoy!

Resources

1. Adair, Bergen. Future of Electronic Medical Records: Experts Predict EMR Trends in 2020. *Select Hub*, undated. https://www.selecthub.com/medical-software/emr/electronic-medical-records-future-emr-trends/. Accessed January 24, 2020.
2. A false claim is an attempt to get the federal and state government to pay money to anyone who is not intended to benefit. Federal and state prosecutors often use the False Claims Act to combat healthcare fraud and abuse.
3. Radick, Robert. Does "Meaningful Use" Mean Widespread Abuse? HHS-OIG's Review of EHR Incentive Payments. *Forbes*, June 30, 2017. https://www.forbes.com/sites/insider/2017/06/30/does-meaningful-use-mean-widespread-abuse-hhs-oigs-review-of-ehr-incentive-payments/#22baae543f02. Accessed January 24, 2020.

About the Authors

Jeffery Daigrepont, senior vice president of Coker Group, specializes in healthcare automation, system integration, operations and the deployment of enterprise information systems for sizable integrated delivery networks. As an admired national speaker, Jeffery is frequently engaged by highly respected organizations across the nation, including non-profit trade associations and state medical societies.

Jeffery is a co-author of *Complete Guide and Toolkit to Successful EHR Adoption* (© HIMSS, 2011) and a contributor to *The Healthcare Executive's Guide to ACO Strategy* (© HCPro, 2012). He is a notable authority and resource for various national media outlets and is frequently quoted in industry publications.

Active in HIMSS for many years, Jeffery is a former chair of the Ambulatory Information Systems Steering Committee. Also, as the Ambulatory Committee liaison for FY09 to the ACEC Planning Committee, he represented the HIMSS Ambulatory and AISC members. Daigrepont is credentialed by the American Academy of Medical Management (AAMM) with an Executive Fellowship in Practice Management (EFMP). He also serves as an independent investment advisor to many of the nation's noteworthy healthcare venture capital firms such as Kleiner Perkins Caufield & Byers (KPCB) and Silver Lake Partners. Contact Jeffery at jdaigrepont@cokergroup.com.

Gabriel Harry is a senior manager in the information technology service line at Coker Group, with 20 years of experience working on a variety of healthcare and IT consulting projects. Gabriel is passionate about using technology to improve clinical outcomes in healthcare environments. He is proficient in best practices in healthcare information technology and the research/development of current technologies to maximize efficiencies and minimize cost. Gabriel's expertise includes a strong delivery of efficient design, implementation, evaluation and outcomes assessment. He has excellent interpersonal, communication and writing skills. Contact Gabriel at gharry@cokergroup.com.

Denise McNairy-Dixon is a staff consultant on the information technology team at Coker Group. She has over 15 years of experience working with clients in telecommunications, healthcare and information technology, assisting in areas such as human resources, hardware/software implementation, staff training, operations and management.

Denise has led the design, development and delivery of multi-dimensional cross-functional solutions to clients, including strategy, business process design, organizational design, process automation, acquisition and implementation of new technology. She helps clients with the selection and implementation of EHR systems and operational management processes, as well as vendor contract reviews and negotiations. Contact Denise at dmcnairydixon@cokergroup.com.

Christopher Torregosa is a vice president with the Coker HIT team, specializing in healthcare automation, with emphasis on practice management and electronic health records software applications. Chris works on a variety of high-level consulting projects, assisting clients in technology assessments and selection, providing guidance and solutions and executing and coordinating strategic project deliverables. He holds a Bachelor of Biological Sciences degree from Rowan University, an Athena Health Client project lead certification, and a Collector, Clinicals and Communication Project Management. Contact Christopher at ctorregosa@cokergroup.com.

Connor Schweik is an associate on the HCIT team with Coker Group. His role is to develop project plans that fit the client's needs and goals. He uses his experience in vendor contracting to serve Coker's clients and achieve optimal results in negotiations, contracting and efficiency. Connor has championed significant projects at the corporate level as an administrator for large healthcare organizations in the Dallas/Fort Worth Metroplex. He holds a Master of Healthcare Administration from the University of North Texas Health Science Center and a Bachelor of Healthcare Administration from the University of Texas at Dallas. He brings that valuable experience as an additional resource, working with the HCIT team to deliver HCIT vendor contracting services, EHR/EMR implementation support, project management and telemedicine solutions. Contact Connor at cschweik@cokergroup.com.

Acronyms

AAFP	American Association of Family Physicians
ACO	Accountable Care Organization
AHIMA	American Health Information Management Association
AI	Artificial intelligence
AMA	American Medical Association
ANSI	American National Standards Institute
API	Application program interface
ARRA	American Recovery and Reinvestment Act of 2009
ASCII	American Standard Code for Information Exchange
ASP	Application service provider
ATA	American Telemedicine Association
AWS	Amazon Web Services
CAH	Critical access hospital
CCHIT	Certification Commission for Health Information Technology
CCPA	California Consumer Privacy Act
CDC	Centers for Disease Control and Prevention
CEHRT	Certified EHR technology
CEO	Chief executive officer
CMO	Chief Medical Officer
CMS	Centers for Medicare and Medicaid Services
CNM	Certified nurse-midwife
DBV	Design, build and validation
DIMS	Document imaging management system
EDI	Electronic data interchange
EHR	Electronic health record
EMR	Electronic medical record
EP	Eligible professional
E-Prescribing	Electronic prescribing

ERD	Entity relationship diagram
FQHC	Federally qualified health center
GUI	Graphical user interface
HCIT	Healthcare information technology
HIE	Health information exchange
HIMSS	Healthcare Information and Management Systems Society
HIPAA	Health Insurance Portability and Accountability Act of 1996
HIS	Hospital information system
HITECH	Health Information Technology for Economic and Clinical Health Act of 2009
IaaS	Infrastructure as a service
IOM	Institute of Medicine
IP	Internet protocol
IT	Information technology
MACRA	Medicare Access and CHIP Reauthorization Act
MIPS	Merit-Based Incentive Payment System
MRI	Medical Records Institute
MU	Meaningful Use
NPI	National Provider Identifier
NPPES	National Plan and Provider Enumeration System
ONC	Office of the National Coordinator for Health Information Technology
PA	Physician assistant
PaaS	Platform as a service
PACS	Picture archiving and communication system
PECOS	Provider enrollment, chain and ownership system
PHI	Personal health information
PM	Practice management
PMI	Project Management Institute
PMO	Project management office
PQRI	Physicians Quality Reporting Initiative
RFI	Request for information
RFP	Request for proposal
RHC	Rural health clinic
ROI	Return on investment
RTF	Rich text format
SaaS	Software as a service
SLA	Service level agreement
SME	Subject-matter expert

SRA   Security risk analysis
VOC   Vendor of choice
VPN   Virtual private network

Introduction

Beyond EHR: Using Technology to Meet Growing Demands and Deliver Better Patient Care assumes the reader has adopted an EHR system. However, if you are new on the scene and searching for information, the precursor to this book, *Complete Guide and Toolkit to Successful EHR Adoption*, is a helpful complement to this information. It is common for a practice or hospital to be on their second or third EHR, often at no fault of the buyer, or there may be a system migration ahead. To that end, this book will include a discussion of EHR-to-EHR conversion. All IT systems will eventually have an end-of-life event and fade into obsolescence. It's just the nature of technology. An example of a technology lifecycle is what we use to enjoy music. The illustration of listening devices, below, puts this progression into perspective.[1]

| Gramophone 1887 | Electric Turntable 1927 | 8-Track 1965 | Cassette 1963 | CD 1982 | MP3 1998 |

Although the IT lifecycle is a disrupter, newer technology across all sectors generally delivers improvements in performance and capabilities. In some areas of technology, especially with processors and microchips, performance and speed have doubled *every two years* since 1970. Yes, doubled! This theory is known as Moore's law, named after Gordon Moore, co-founder of Intel.[2] Some have suggested we are nearing a rate of saturation (reaching peak performance), and there has been some recent indication of this phenomenon slowing down, but the trend mostly holds to this day.

For some, this rapid change might mean upgrading an existing EHR and migrating data into a new system. For others, it could mean enhancing what you have. It might mean incorporating and even innovating new technology, such as artificial intelligence, telemedicine, advanced reporting, electronic patient engagement and the like.

The goal of this book is to pick up where most EHRs have been over the past five years, which is mostly as a lone electronic repository of data limited to a single entity/provider. To achieve the original goals and objectives for mandating the use of EHRs, we now must focus on interoperability and patient engagement, with patient safety, quality and improved outcomes as our top priority.

We will examine the ways we can enhance and improve the end-user and patient experience without sacrificing the personal nature of providing personal care. We will explore ways to leverage technology to help solve some of our significant challenges, such as provider shortage, patient access and an aging population. Finally, we will address the unexpected COVID-19 crisis and how healthcare technology has come front and center in our response to this crisis.

As the economic landscape continues shifting toward value, technology, specifically data, will become critical to demonstrate positive outcomes and/or factors to influence behavior for both the provider and patient. Our journey will cover a variety of topics in concert with many of the fundamentals from the first edition. Specific issues we will address are as follows:

Current state of the market
Cloud computing
Cybersecurity
Compliance
Artificial intelligence
Electronic patient engagement
EHRs and telemedicine
Advance analytics and dashboard reporting
Interoperability
Vendor contracting
Implementation and project management
Future trends and Internet of things
Appendix A: Tools and policies
Appendix B: Acronyms

Our goal is to provide those who are ready to go beyond EHR with some guidance and inspiration on what is possible, but also point out lessons learned and proven strategies. Technology evolves rapidly, so we tried to include links to many resources that are frequently kept up to date with the latest policies.

In closing, technology will never replace the provider–patient relationship we have all come to value and appreciate, but the right technology in the hands of great leadership can be truly transformational. The following quote from Steve Jobs best captures this opinion:

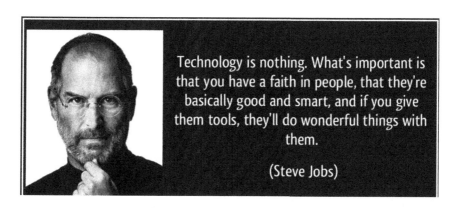

Technology is nothing. What's important is that you have a faith in people, that they're basically good and smart, and if you give them tools, they'll do wonderful things with them.

(Steve Jobs)

Resources

1. Listening devices:
   Gramophone: www.needpix.com/photo/529065/nostalgia-gramophone-recor d-music-playback-device-grooves-speakers-sound-acoustics.Electric turntable: https://commons.wikimedia.org/wiki/File:Philips_212_Electronic_Turntable. jpg.8 track player: https://commons.wikimedia.org/wiki/File:Vintage_Panaso nic_8_Track_Tape_Player,_The_Dynamite_8,_Model_RQ-830S,_Produced_In_ Blue,_Red_%26_Yellow_Colors,_Made_In_Japan,_Circa_1974_(21317771872).jpg .Cassette player: https://en.wikipedia.org/wiki/File:RadioShack-ctr-119.jpg.CD player: https://commons.wikimedia.org/wiki/File:Discman_D121.jpg.MP3 player: https://pixabay.com/vectors/ipod-music-mp3-player-mp3-songs-297232/.
2. www.investopedia.com/terms/m/mooreslaw.asp. Accessed May 1, 2020.

Chapter 1

The Current State of the Healthcare IT Market

According to the Office of the National Coordinator (ONC), the term "health information technology" (health IT) refers to the electronic systems healthcare professionals – and, increasingly, patients – use to store, share and analyze health information. Health IT includes electronic health records (EHRs), but it can be much more comprehensive.[1] For these reasons, it will be helpful first to understand the current state of the healthcare IT (HCIT) market and how it drives new applications that go beyond the way we use EHRs today.

The most notable state of our current HCIT market has to do with incentives and penalties for the use and adoption of certified EHRs. This matter will be covered in more detail later in the book. Still, for a quick contrast and comparison, the original EHR incentive program started under the **American Recovery and Reinvestment Act of 2009** during the Obama administration. Our economy was teetering on the brink of a second Great Depression, and we desperately needed incentives to stimulate the economy. One of the largest benefactors of this bill was the healthcare IT sector. Over $20 billion in incentive money was allocated to encourage the adoption of a certified EHR.[2]

Prior to Obama, the Stark Laws were relaxed under the Bush administration during his second term to allow hospitals to subsidize the cost of EHRs for their medical staff. These combined, back-to-back efforts jumpstarted the adoption of EHRs. The program developed under the Affordable Care Act was mostly based on adoption and selecting a vendor with certified features and functions. (Note: The Patient Protection and Affordable Care Act, also the Affordable Care Act or colloquially known as Obamacare, is a United States federal statute enacted by the 111th United States Congress and signed into law by President Barack Obama on March 23, 2010.) To be eligible, doctors and hospitals only had to pick a certified vendor and attest to using the basic features of the EHR. There were no major conditions or attempts to verify. This created a mass explosion of new vendors rushing to get their share of these funds. At the apex, there were over 600 certified EHRs in the market. Most of these vendors no longer exist and/or have since merged with other vendors to remain viable.

Today, the incentive programs are more comprehensive and require some demonstrated outcomes. Table 1.1 gives a quick side-by-side comparison of the incentives. Figures 1.1 and 1.2 recap the first calendar year for which the EP receives an incentive payment.

Fast forward to 2020, MIPS and MACRA have replaced Meaningful Use, and there is increased scrutiny and auditing of both vendors and providers who benefited from the former incentive programs. Most notably, three major vendors were hit with major false claim violations from the DOJ, resulting in a multimillion-dollar settlement with the government. Providers and hospitals are being asked to submit documentation demonstrating they complied with all the conditions sworn to during the attestation process. (Note: Attestation is a process of making a claim/statement without the requirement of submitting supporting documentation to validate these claims/statements. The government accepts these statements without verification but reserves the right to audit at any time to ensure the statements are accurate.)

Those who cannot produce the documentation are forced to return the incentive money. CMS will deduct the funds from future reimbursement and/or may impose additional fines for failing to comply. One of the conditions most frequently missed is the security risk analysis (SRA).[3] (Note: Measure: Conduct or review a security risk analysis in accordance with the requirements under 45 CFR 164.308(a)(1), including addressing the security (including encryption) of data created or maintained by CEHRT in accordance with requirements under 45 CFR 164.312(a)(2)(iv) and 45.)

This SRA is a pass/fail measure, so it is a manageable condition for HHS to audit. Practices that do not produce evidence of performing an annual SRA are generally asked to return the incentive money. The practice, to pass an SRA, must have all its HIPAA privacy and security policies current and provide evidence of staff training and TESTING of their knowledge. Table 1.2 outlines instructions to help you conduct a risk analysis that is

Table 1.1 Original and Current Incentives Compared

Original EHR Incentives	Current EHR Incentives
• The vendor must be certified by the Certification Commission for Healthcare Information Technology (CCHIT).	• The Certification Commission for Healthcare Information Technology (CCHIT).
• Meet Meaningful Use (MU) standards MU was based on five main objectives, according to the Centers for Disease Control and Prevention. They were: (1) Improve quality (2) Safety (3) Efficiency (4) Reduce health disparities (5) Increase patient engagement	• Meaningful Use +++ MU has now shifted to a Merit-Based Incentive Payment System and is combined with the Medicare Access and CHIP Reauthorization Act (MACRA); the Medicare EHR Incentive Program, commonly referred to as Meaningful Use, was transitioned to become one of the four components of the new Merit-Based Incentive Payment System (MIPS), which itself is part of MACRA. MIPS harmonizes existing CMS quality programs (including Meaningful Use), the Physician Quality Reporting System and Value-Based Payment Modifiers. MIPS consolidates multiple quality programs into a single program to improve quality care.
• Compensation The payout was over 5 stages with phase one starting with 15 core requirements and 10 menu requirements. All core requirements are mandatory. Additional core requirements were added each year by CMS. There were two payout tracks. 1. Medicare Track: Eligible providers could receive up to $44,000 if all stages for all years were met. (See Figure 1.1.) 2. Medicaid Track: Eligible providers could receive up to $63,750. The only requirement for phase one was a signed contract with a certified vendor. The requirements for Medicaid were lower because Medicaid practices have less access to capital. To qualify for the Medicaid track, the provider would have to have a minimum of 30% Medicaid patients. (See Figure 1.2.)	• Compensation as an up or down adjustment to the provider's Medicare payments. The first year started at a plus or minus of 4%, and it is set to go up to plus or minus 9% by 2021. Additional incentives can be gained through alternative payment models, but the risk is higher.

- First Calendar Year (CY) for which the EP Receives an Incentive Payment

	CY 2011	CY 2012	CY 2013	CY2014	CY 2015 and later
CY 2011	$18,000				
CY 2012	$12,000	$18,000			
CY 2013	$8,000	$12,000	$15,000		
CY 2014	$4,000	$8,000	$12,000	$12,000	
CY 2015	$2,000	$4,000	$8,000	$8,000	$0
CY 2016		$2,000	$4,000	$4,000	$0
TOTAL	$44,000	$44,000	$39,000	$24,000	$0

Figure 1.1   Original MU payout – Medicare. Source: CMS.

Maximum Incentive Payments for Medicaid EPs Who Are Meaningful Users in the First Payment Year

		Medicaid EPs who begin MU of certified EHR technology in					
		2011	2012	2013	2014	2015	2016
Calendar Year	2011	$21,250					
	2012	$8,500	$21,250				
	2013	$8,500	$8,500	$21,250			
	2014	$8,500	$8,500	$8,500	$21,250		
	2015	$8,500	$8,500	$8,500	$8,500	$21,250	
	2016	$8,500	$8,500	$8,500	$8,500	$8,500	$21,250
	2017		$8,500	$8,500	$8,500	$8,500	$8,500
	2018			$8,500	$8,500	$8,500	$8,500
	2019				$8,500	$8,500	$8,500
	2020					$8,500	$8,500
	2021						$8,500
	Total	$63,750	$63,750	$63,750	$63,750	$63,750	$63,750

Figure 1.2   Original MU Medicaid payout. Source: CMS.

appropriate for your organization. Extensive information is available at www. hhs.gov/hipaa/for-professionals/security/index.html.

Conducting a HIPAA Security Rule Risk Analysis

The first requirement of the HIPAA Security Rule is a risk analysis (updated in 2013 by the Omnibus Rule). Per 164.308(a)(1)(ii)(A), a CE or BA must

Table 1.2 Checklist for Conducting a HIPAA Security Rule Risk Analysis

Task	Completed
Define the scope of the risk analysis and collect data regarding the ePHI pertinent to the defined scope.	
Identify potential threats and vulnerabilities to patient privacy and to the security of your practice's ePHI.	
Assess the effectiveness of implemented security measures in protecting against the identified threats and vulnerabilities.	
Determine the likelihood a particular threat will occur and the impact such an occurrence would have on the confidentiality, integrity and availability of ePHI.	
Determine and assign risk levels based on the likelihood and impact of a threat occurrence.	
Prioritize the remediation or mitigation of identified risks based on the severity of their impact on your patients and practice.	
Document your risk analysis, including information from the steps above, as well as the risk analysis results.	
Review and update your risk analysis periodically.	

"conduct an accurate and thorough assessment of the potential risks and vulnerabilities to the confidentiality, integrity, and availability of electronic protected health information (ePHI) held by the covered entity or business associate."[3]

While there is no preferred approach, most risk analysis and risk management processes have steps in common. In concurrence with CMS, Table 1.2 is a checklist of recommended actions.

Additionally, an SRA tip sheet is available at www.cms.gov/Regulations-and-Guidance/Legislation/EHRIncentivePrograms/Downloads/2016_SecurityRiskAnalysis.pdf.

Emerging New Markets

Moving beyond the trends of incentives and auditing, we are now seeing emerging new markets of innovation enabling caregivers to go beyond their internal EHRs. The push for interoperability has moved the market toward an application programming interface (API) model. An application programming interface is an interface or communication protocol between a client and a server intended to simplify the building of client-side software. The best example of an API strategy is in companies like Apple Inc, Amazon, Google and others.

Apple, for example, provides its platform (operating system) as the framework, but it opened its API to anyone who wants to develop an application to run on its platform. Amazon now has a global distribution network allowing retailers from all over the globe to have a platform to promote their goods and services. Amazon has also opened Amazon Web Services (AWS) along with its API so that developers can have interoperability, and they can have full use of the Amazon data center. (Note: Amazon Web Services is a subsidiary of Amazon that provides on-demand cloud computing platforms to individuals, companies and governments, on a metered pay-as-you-go basis.)

Most of the major vendors that had previously offered their EHRs installed on on-premises servers located on-site at the practice are now operating on the Amazon (or similar) cloud platforms. These tech giants are disrupting the old model of isolated systems running as on-premises silos. They also have provisions in their agreements that allow for data mining, which some say is becoming the new currency. In short, the trend is to have an entire ecosystem of applications, all pointing back to a central platform that is accessible from anywhere there is an Internet connection. As a result, millions of private innovators are building and developing applications across a myriad of markets and verticals, including healthcare.

Another major trend is the concept of an open API, which is when a software development allows the open market to have integration with its platform/operating system. An API is a set of routines, protocols and tools for building software applications. Basically, an API specifies how software components should interact. Also, APIs are used when programming graphical user interface (GUI) components. The best example of this concept is the App Store provided by some of the largest cell phone device manufacturers such as Apple and Android. Millions of applications are built to run on these devices. As a result, the consumer becomes dependent on the device because it is necessary in order to run the applications.

Creating this ecosystem drives consumers to the devices supporting their favorite apps. It also makes it particularly challenging to change a device because it often means giving up many of the applications designed for these devices. Major vendors such as EPIC, CERNER, Allscripts, Athena and others have taken notice and recently started publishing their API to encourage the private market to develop solutions to enhance their platforms and the end-user's experience. This action not only creates an ecosystem of solutions, but it also speeds up development and lowers cost by allowing third-party companies to do innovation as a complement to the core EHR platform. It is also an excellent strategy to tie the consumer to a product the provider depends on, thus creating a complete ecosystem. That said, unlike Apple and Amazon, EHR vendors can still be very proprietary and selective with who they allow to access their API.

The EHR vendor may even attempt to block access if the application competes with any of the inherent features and functions already provided by the EHR vendors and/or an existing partner. Some EHR vendors will create a "developer-approved" marketplace and only allow innovators who agree to share in revenue to get their endorsements as a preferred partner/application. While it is understandable for an EHR vendor to align exclusively with innovators who best support their objectives, there may be instances where the practices/hospitals want/need interoperability outside of the core EHR vendor's ecosystem of application. Later, we will discuss how to address this in the vendor-contracting process, but the short answer could mean additional cost. The EHR vendor will most likely impose a fee of $10,000 to $20,000 to develop an interface that doesn't already exist, or, worse, it may deny the request altogether.

With the movement to the API model, the industry has seen remarkable innovation since the introduction of EHRs 20 years ago. The improvements in Internet speeds/access, cloud computing and Web-enabled solutions have been major accelerators in this growth. Many thought EHR spending/investing would be the extent of their spending, but the market continues to expand and evolve. The next section will provide some insights into this anticipated growth.

Projected Growth

As the world changes and technology progresses, hospitals and other medical professionals must do the same. As the technology in the world has expanded, the healthcare IT market has skyrocketed, and with it, the reach of hospitals/medical practices. Projections are that the market worth will climb sharply to $324.9 billion by 2026, an astronomical growth from the $187.9 billion it is at right now in 2019.[4] Figure 1.3 charts the projected increase in the marketplace.

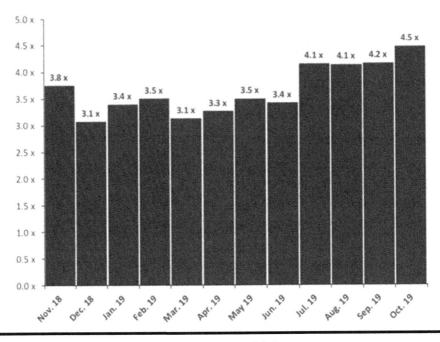

Latest Twelve Month ("LTM") Public Co. Multiples:
Average Enterprise Value ("EV") / LTM Revenue by Month |

Figure 1.3   Latest 12-month public company multiples.

With the growing market, hospitals and medical professionals have had to make and will be making many critical decisions to ensure that they continue to grow as the market grows. One of the most significant decisions hospitals and other medical professionals must make now is selecting the next phase of IT investing. For some, it will be starting over and replacing their old, commercially discontinued EHR. These practices/hospitals will have to grapple with the data migration options/cost. Some may turn to third-party options such as data-archiving solutions, to retire their legacy systems. For others, it will be building/expanding off their existing platforms and exploring innovation. Some examples include the following:

- Telemedicine
- Telemedicine with clinical chatbot support
- Advanced electronic patient communication

As technology has changed, and medicine has progressed, patients now have a greater desire to engage with their health and change their lives to improve their health. Some of the tools these patients are incorporating into their daily lifestyle are basic fitness apps on their phones and fitness watches like Fitbits, Apple Watches or other smartwatches. The applications on their phone, such as the Health app or MyFitnessPal, track the person's activity and workouts, which enables the users to decide whether their caloric needs are sufficient to ensure a healthy lifestyle. The users can also enter the food they eat, which helps them see how they are eating and determine whether they are meeting their caloric needs, exceeding them or falling behind on them. These fitness watches track all motion, not just workouts, and give the users an accurate measure of their daily movement and calories burned, which allows them to view a typical day and see what foods to eat and which ones to avoid. These tools assist physicians with patients because they now have an accurate measure of the patients' activity, which allows them to find faults in their daily lifestyle and prescribe changes that fit the patients' shortcomings. By having a detailed record of the patient's lifestyle, the physician can prescribe specific changes, whether it is to diet or exercise, before prescribing a medication. Even if the physician must prescribe medicine, they can give one that works best with the patient and their daily life. Research in the emergency department indicates about 90% of people would be interested in incorporating these tools in their lives, yet they are seldom used. Why is that?

Some of the concerns of these tools include privacy and security and worries about them being ineffective. With recent security breaches in companies like Facebook, consumers are worried about putting more personal information into technology. This concern is valid yet should not hold consumers back. Technology, as it expands, will be at the center of growth, and information will end up online or in some sort of technology at a continually increasing rate. Also, many of the creators of the apps have installed robust security protocols that make hacking and stealing information extremely difficult. The concern about effectiveness is an argument often presented by those who oppose the change to a more technology-based world. However, technology will progress; those who resist will have the option to go along with the changes or fall behind. As medicine progresses and the market grows, all medical professionals must incorporate these technologies into their practices so that they can accurately diagnose patients. By incorporating these tools into their daily lives, patients can take charge of their health and improve on their own rather than requiring a physician for every step. Incorporating patient engagement tools into daily practice ensures a larger pool of patients for physicians.

Another aspect of the growing healthcare IT market is the increased use and prominence of artificial intelligence (AI). As diseases and illnesses change and evolve, medical professionals must have a system to track them and how they have changed on a molecular level. Here, AI enters the picture because it can quickly analyze data and help physicians find patterns. This pattern recognition helps medical professionals and researchers see where, how and why a disease is changing. Identifying these factors can help physicians treat diseases with proper prescriptions and can help researchers discover a cure sooner.[5]

Rather than analyzing data by hand, which could take days, scientists can insert those data into the system for instant analysis. This analysis helps with looking for cures for diseases such as cancer and certain neural issues. One of the pioneer AI systems in use is IBM Watson. Watson is an IBM supercomputer that combines AI and sophisticated analytical software for optimal performance as a "question-answering" machine. The supercomputer is named for IBM's founder, Thomas J. Watson. Watson can process data within seconds and help scientists find trends and patterns in data instantly. By incorporating these systems into medical practices, medical professionals are better able to analyze patient data and find patient patterns faster, rather than going through all the data by hand. AI systems significantly speed up data analysis for scientists, which can help them find cures more rapidly, which then helps medical professionals treat more patients. AI also speeds up medical practices, which leads to more efficient work from doctors. The increased use of AI has contributed significantly to the current trend in the healthcare IT market due to its increased efficiency.

Most people lead busy lives, and many of them choose not to see physicians because they do not have the time or money. Instead, they believe that they can self-treat by using Google and WebMD as their resource. However, the marketplace is experiencing a growth in the use of telemedicine. Telemedicine is the communication between medical professionals and their patients through a two-way device. Doctors can now treat patients remotely, whether from the comfort of their home or their practice. With the growing healthcare IT market, telemedicine is increasingly popular because people no longer have to go somewhere for treatment; they can receive care in the comfort of their own home.[6,7]

Even ambulances now include telemedicine. When there is an emergency, and a patient is being transported to the hospital, the paramedics can use Bluetooth stethoscopes. Doctors can hear the heartbeat from the hospital, find the most effective treatment before the sick or injured person arrives, and administer rapid treatment. Telemedicine will contribute to the future growth of the healthcare IT market because Generation Z relies on technology. Thus, they will participate in telemedicine more than previous generations. The doubling of the market value will mainly be due to telemedicine, in which many of the younger generations will join. For doctors and other medical professionals to change with the times and progress with the market, they will have to incorporate more telemedicine into their practices. The more they offer the option for telemedicine, the more patients they will attract, which will then contribute to their growth as a practice and contribute more to the expanding market.

As the healthcare IT market shifts and develops, medical professionals must recognize what is changing the market so that they can incorporate these tools into their practices. Along with selecting the correct EHR system, they must include a variety of other resources that are currently contributing to the growth of the market. Integrating patient engagement tools, artificial intelligence and telemedicine into their practices will enable them to grow along with the healthcare IT market. As the market begins to increase and double, it is up to hospitals to incorporate these resources to keep up with the demand.[8]

Predictions

Although Chapter 12 addresses future market trends, the following are some useful and wacky predictions:

■ **A hospital at home**. The hospital of the future may be in the comfort of your own home. This concept is currently being developed and tested by the Johns Hopkins Schools of Medicine and the Public Health Departments in some markets. Expectations are that this innovative care model will lower costs by nearly one-third and reduce complications. So far, patients and caregivers alike have given positive feedback.

■ **Ambulance ride services similar to assistances such as Uber and Lyft**. The high cost of an ambulance service is not in transportation. The ambulance comes with a fully trained emergency medical team and expensive lifesaving equipment, when, in many cases, the patient just needs a ride to the ER. Both Uber and Lyft are investigating creating a rideshare option where the driver is a qualified caregiver for non-trauma type events.

- **The chatbot will see you now**. We alluded to this previously, but several companies are now creating chatbots that can treat patients based on algorithms and responses to Q&A. There is also technology under development that can pick up stress/pain signals in a patient's voice to determine if the care requires escalation.
- **Self-treating pathways for consumers**. For example, you have a child with a chronic ear infection, and the parent knows it is an ear infection based on the previous ten ear infections. The parent generally knows what is necessary to treat it or could follow a past procedure. For uncomplicated problems such as an ear infection, there could be an at-home diagnostic tool that would confirm what the parent already knows, then open secure access to treatment delivered directly to the home.
- **Digital phenotyping**. *Phenotypes* are physical traits such as eye or hair color, height, voice, shoe size and the like, influenced by *genotypes. Phenotyping* is when these traits are used in clinical research for the discovery of diseases. In the digital era, researchers have joined hands with technology companies to monitor how people interact with the digital world to understand their mood, cognition and behavior. Major technology companies, such as Google, Amazon, Facebook and Netflix, are already tracking and storing mass quantities of data on every click we make online, including monitoring our movement and private messages. Consider the scenario that someone with a highly social digital phenotype one day goes dark and isolated.

  Perhaps, they are now exploring a website that deals with depression or suicide or watching videos that promote violence or school shootings. Could this be used to help with early intervention before someone gets hurt, or is this an invasion of privacy? You may have already seen that your phone can tell you exactly how you spent your time online down to what apps you spent the most time on, so the data are being captured. The question is, how will it be used, and can we balance the good with the need to protect privacy rights?
- **Wearables**. Devices we wear on our bodies already exist, but they will become increasingly advanced and include more interoperability with our caregivers.
- **A spoon full or microchip**. A digital pill is a capsule like any pill today, but it contains an ingestible sensor inside it. The sensor begins transmitting medical data after it is consumed. The technology that

makes up the pill, as well as the data transmitted by the pill's sensor, is part of digital medicine. The FDA has recently approved such a device, but we have not researched the best way to return it when it exits the digestive system.

Summary

Writing a chapter about HCIT market trends is one of the best ways to create cringe-worthy content ten years from now. There is no way of knowing where today's and tomorrow's technologies will take us; nonetheless, it will be very disruptive. As we reflect on the last ten years since the first edition of this book was published, we have learned many lessons that we will apply in this edition. We know that despite all the best efforts to date, healthcare cost continues to rise, and access continues to worsen. While healthcare IT will not solve all challenges, it will play a significant role and is expected to become even more prolific within our healthcare delivery system and personal lives. The opportunities and possibilities are endless, given the challenges we face today. As you go beyond EHR, we encourage becoming active in HIMSS, as it allows you access to a network of peers and innovators willing to share their knowledge and experience. This challenge is not something any one of us can surmount alone. We must come together, exchange ideas and learn from each other.

Resources

1. Market Watch. Press Release: Healthcare IT 2019 Global Market Net Worth US$ 324.9 Billion Forecast By 2026, January 29, 2019. https://www.marketwatch.com/press-release/healthcare-it-2019-global-market-net-worth-us-3249-billion-forecast-by-2026-2019-01-29. Accessed January 23, 2020.
2. H.R.1 - American Recovery and Reinvestment Act of 2009111th Congress (2009–2010). https://www.congress.gov/bill/111th-congress/house-bill/1/text. Accessed May 1, 2020.
3. Department of Health and Human Services. Guidance on Risk Analysis. https://www.hhs.gov/hipaa/for-professionals/security/guidance/guidance-risk-analysis/index.html. Accessed May 1, 2020.
4. Markets and Markets. Press Release: Healthcare IT Market worth $390.7 billion by 2024. https://www.marketsandmarkets.com/PressReleases/healthcare-it-market.asp. Accessed January 23, 2020.

5. Daly, Sam. "Surgical Robots, New Medicines and Better Care: 32 Examples of AI in Healthcare." *Built-In*, March 25, 2020. https://builtin.com/artificial-intelligence/artificial-intelligence-healthcare. Accessed May 1, 2020.
6. Jiang, Fei, Jiang, Yong, Zhi, Hui, Dong, Yi, Li, Hao, Ma, Sufeng, Wang, Yilong, Dong, Qiang, Shen, Haipeng, Wang, Yongjun. Artificial Intelligence in Healthcare: Past, Present and Future. *Stroke and Vascular Neurology, BMJ Journals*. https://svn.bmj.com/content/2/4/230.abstract. Accessed January 23, 2020.
7. Bazolli, Fred. Health Data Management. 12 Trends that will Dominate Healthcare IT in 2019. https://www.healthdatamanagement.com/list/12-trends-that-will-dominate-healthcare-it-in-2019. Accessed January 23, 2020.
8. Birnbaum, F, Lewis, D.M., Rosen, R., Ranney, M.L. Patient Engagement and the Design Of Digital Health. *PMC*. Published online May 21, 2015. doi:10.1111/acem.12692. https://www.ncbi.nlm.nih.gov/pmc/articles/PMC4674428/. Accessed January 23, 2020.

Chapter 2

Cloud Computing

Cloud computing is the concept of delivering software over the Internet. This concept has been a growing trend across all industry sectors over the last decade as Internet cost, availability and speeds have improved dramatically. The opportunity that cloud computing offers and questions of why and how to get there are open for debate and often mischaracterized by vendors. The most common misinterpretation of cloud computing is that it is an on-premises system hosted in a data center. Vendors will often call this cloud computing because the server is managed in a data center and accessed over the Internet. This is not true cloud computing. It is just the equivalent of an on-premises server managed off-site. On-**premises** software (also known as on-**premise** and abbreviated "on-**prem**") is installed and runs on computers on the **premises** of the person or organization using the software, rather than at a remote facility such as a server farm or cloud.

The correct definition of this scenario is a *hosted* system, and the software would be a **single instance** exclusive to one client. A "single instance" means a copy of a running program. In contrast, cloud computing is **multitenant**, shared by many users. Multitenant architecture, commonly referred to as multitenancy, is a software architecture in which multiple single instances of software run on a single physical server. The server then serves multiple tenants.

A non-technical example would be like comparing a condo to a single-family home, as in Table 2.1.

Several adoption strategies are emerging as healthcare providers evaluate the benefits and disadvantages of cloud-based solutions. Implementing the right strategy is critical when determining your future-readiness, especially

Table 2.1 Comparison of Single vs Shared Networks

Multitenant Pros and Cons	Single Instance Pros and Cons
PRO: Residents share costs.	**CON:** One owner bears all costs.
CON: Ability to modify is limited due to the potential of impacting everyone sharing the system.	**PRO:** Modifications are usually allowed.
PRO: Typically has stronger, more robust cybersecurity measures since the cost is shared across many users, including nightly back-ups and disaster recovery.	**CON:** Responsible for all aspects of cybersecurity, disaster recovery, back-ups and monitoring.
CON: Depends on a robust and reliable Internet connection.	**PRO:** Can access system without Internet.
PRO: Updates, server upgrades and refresh are included.	**CON:** Requires reinvestment of capital every 3 to 5 years.
CON: System access and return of data. Vendor could disable access in the event of a dispute or shutdown. (See Chapter 10 on vendor contracting for how to minimize this risk.)	**PRO:** Owner has complete control of system access and data.

as healthcare increasingly becomes information-driven and moves toward collaborative-care models and payment reform.

According to the U.S. National Institute of Standards and Technology, cloud computing is:

> a model for enabling ubiquitous, convenient, on-demand network access to a shared pool of configurable computing resources (e.g.,

networks, servers, storage, applications, and services) that can be rapidly provisioned and released with minimal management effort or service provider interaction.[1]

The greatest advantage of cloud computing is that expensive on-premises servers, software, and networking equipment are no longer needed when subscribing to a solution delivered through the cloud. However, as stated previously, the term "cloud computing" is often mischaracterized and can be a buzzword used as a marketing gimmick. Buyers should be aware that not all cloud-based solutions are created equal. Here are a few concepts related to gaining access to software that can guide you when distinguishing between the different types of options that are somewhat like true cloud computing.

- **Infrastructure as a service (IaaS)**. Under this method, the medical practice owns the software, though it is installed and operated at a remote data center. The practice pays for disk space used or a monthly rental fee based on the number of servers/racks. The data center provider and the software vendor are not the same company.
- **Platform as a service (PaaS)**. The PaaS option generally builds on the IaaS model, but it stacks several solutions together into one monthly fee. This bundle could include the operating system, hardware, software, storage and other fees. In this arrangement, one provider manages all the solutions, but the solutions may come from different vendors.
- **Software as a service (SaaS)**. With SaaS, the software vendor is also the hosting provider. There is typically a monthly subscription fee that includes software, hosting, storage, backups and all the IT support related to the software.
- **Traditional hosting/application service provider**. This arrangement may include any third-party company that takes what is normally installed and managed on premise and provides the same service off-site. In this arrangement, the traditional client/server configuration stays the same; however, it is managed off site, which can be in a data center or a person's basement. There are not many economic advantages to this option because the technology is still based on the client/server configuration. So, no hard cost is eliminated.

Multitenant vs Single Instance

Another factor to consider with cloud computing is determining whether the solution delivered over the Internet is "multitenant" or "single instance." This factor is essential because it drives value and overall performance. Applications that are multitenant can leverage the benefits of having only one version of its software to support at any given time. It also allows for knowledge sharing and rapid responsiveness to changes in the healthcare landscape.

Facebook is a good example of a multitenant environment. Everyone uses the same version, and when an improvement occurs, everyone benefits simultaneously. Similarly, when an issue or problem surfaces, the vendor only has to correct the problem once; everyone receives the same fix immediately and simultaneously.

By contrast, a cloud-based system built on a single instance of the software still requires each practice to individually address upgrades, new releases, patches, etc. Thus, not as much value is created because the cost is not shared among everyone using the same instance of the software. The same analogy applies to individuals living in a condominium community. When the roof needs replacing, all the tenants share in the cost to replace the one roof. However, everyone must also agree on the same color for the roof, so there are some tradeoffs.

What Are the Risks?

Though there are many benefits with cloud computing, there are also risks and negatives to consider, as in Table 2.2.

Adoption Concerns

Although cloud computing offers significant advantages compared with on-premises models, adoption has been slow to come to healthcare. Hospitals are still mostly managed with on-premises servers due to the critical nature of running a 24/7 operation. Most of the cloud computing adoption to date is in ambulatory practices, which is no surprise considering the limited budget practices have to spend on major on-premises hardware. The most widespread concerns with cloud computing are the loss of control and

Table 2.2 Risks and Concerns with Cloud Computing

Risk	Concern
Data security/ privacy	Since cloud systems typically include massive databases containing millions of patient records within a single instance of software, they are attractive targets for cyber criminals. It is crucial to know who will be responsible and accountable for security breaches. Does your contract with the cloud vendor spell this out? Most contracts put the responsibility back on the practice, even though the cloud vendor promotes security as a benefit. The vendor must be responsible and accountable for any cybersecurity breaches, if they are in compete and total control of the environment. This is the trade-off in this arrangement, and most practices inherently expect the cloud vendor to take responsibility.
Confidentiality	The practice, not the vendor, will be held to the same standards for confidentiality. We recommend verifying protocols and safeguards to protect confidential information. Although the vendor manages the system access, the practice is still expected to demonstrate compliance with all the HIPAA policies, including the responsibility for verifying that the vendor has performed an annual security risk analysis, since they are directly managing protected health information (PHI) on behalf of the practice. **Protected health information** (PHI) under US law is any **information** about **health** status, provision of **health**care or payment for **health**care that is created or collected by a Covered Entity (or a Business Associate of a Covered Entity), and can be linked to a specific individual.
Compliance	As with any software, a cloud-based system is expected to comply with ICD-10, Meaningful Use, vendor certification standards and other compliance standards if the practice intends to comply with many of the Medicare programs, such as the Merit-Based Incentive Payment System (**MIPS**) and the Medicare Access and CHIP Reauthorization Act of 2015 (**MACRA**). (These CMS programs are covered in more detail later in this book.)
Availability	System access and up time are critical concerns. What would you do if a vendor disabled your access to your data? The contract must prohibit vendors from shutting off access without a lengthy notification period and/or opportunity to resolve the issues before they can disable access. The vendor should also provide up-time guarantees for reliability and be willing to provide outage credits for any unscheduled downtime. (Tips for address these concerns can be found in Chapter 10, Vendor Contracting.)

(Continued)

Table 2.2 (Continued) Risks and Concerns with Cloud Computing

Risk	Concern
Service level agreements (SLA)	Support agreements are just as crucial, if not more, with a cloud provider, because you typically do not own the software; you will be relying 100% on their support and responsiveness. Support agreements should also spell out how downtime is managed and testing of future upgrades, since the practice will be completely dependent on the vendor for these matters. One major challenge with cloud vendors is maintaining any unique customization after a major system upgrade. These customizations can get lost when versions change.
Termination	While you never enter into an agreement with plans to terminate, a practice should never purchase cloud services without a clear exit plan that has defined parameters in place. The termination agreement must stipulate system access after termination, return of data and proper storage and archiving of the data after system shutdown. At no time should a vendor be allowed to disable access without proper notice. We recommend 120 days. (Tips to minimize this risk will be covered in Chapter 10 on vendor contracting.)

having access disabled without notice. Other worries include the security and confidentiality of patient information, up time, access, interoperability and compliance with government regulations. Over time, the adoption of cloud computing is expected to increase, as will the confidence level among physicians and practices considering this option.

What Is next?

The current trend indicates that soon we will be using cloud computing exclusively for both business and personal use. Need proof? According to PocketGamer and Statista, Apple's App Store is adding 1,000 new apps per day, which are all delivered via cloud computing.[2] These applications download remotely without any human intervention and can be operational almost instantly. Figure 2.1 illustrates this growth in applications.

The worldwide public cloud services market is projected to grow 17.5% in 2019 to total $214.3 billion, up from $182.4 billion in 2018, according to Gartner, Inc.[3] Many of the vendors in the market today no longer offer an on-premises option, and/or they are in the process of rewriting their

Apple's App Store Is Growing by 1,000+ Apps a Day

Number of new apps submitted to Apple's App Store per month

Figure 2.1   Application growth chart. Source: pocketgamer.biz; @StatistaCharts.

platforms to be cloud-enabled. As Internet speeds and availability continue to improve, it will further fuel the growth of cloud computing. Unknown disrupters include industry giants such as Microsoft at https://azure.microsoft.com/en-us/; Amazon at https://aws.amazon.com/; and Google at https://cloud.google.com/, who are all actively pushing and promoting fully managed cloud services to the market. Today, these platforms are mostly leveraged by vendors that want to avoid the data center cost, yet still be nimble when it comes to innovation and speed to market. Providers such as Amazon are capable of critical mass at a fraction of the cost compared to being self-managed. Some industry experts predict these industry giants will be better positioned for managing the interoperability and patient engagement since they are already digitally connected to so many consumers (aka your patients).

On the privacy and consumer protection front, there is growing concern with how these companies are using and selling our data. Some argue that consumers are benefiting from the use of these platforms, so giving up personal data is an inherent tradeoff. However, a movement is growing to pass laws giving consumers control of their personal data. Specifically, consumer protection agencies are pressuring vendors to allow consumers the right to delete their data. The movement is called the "Right to be Forgotten," but it gets complicated as many of these platforms depend on mass quantities of crowd-sourced data to deliver their services and value to consumers. For example, if you want your phone to tell you where to find the nearest Starbucks, you must give your location for this service to work; hence, the tradeoff dilemma facing consumers and vendors. California has been the first state to pass consumer data rights, which include the right to be deleted. These laws are expected to spread to other states as they are already widely accepted in Europe. For more information on the California Consumer Privacy Act (CCPA), go to https://ccpa-info.com/home/1798-105 -consumers-right-to-deletion/?gclid=EAIaIQobChMIuKvhvseS5gIVwhitBh0peg nZEAAYASAAEgL74vD_BwE.

Summary

Cloud computing will continue to grow in popularity and is steadily becoming the primary way technology is delivered and used. The most critical points to know and consider with any cloud computing vendor are the policies for system access and return of data. Because you do not own the software, knowing your system access rights, including the rights to access the system after termination or in the event of a dispute, is critical. Moreover, YOUR data will reside in an environment you do not own or control, so how it will be returned, archived or used beyond the original intent MUST be understood. These issues can easily be addressed in the contract and should not intimidate anyone from considering cloud computing as an option.

The following online resources will be helpful.

Resources	Links
HIMSS offers a comprehensive set of resources tools to healthcare organizations in terms of risk management, operational integrity and data security in the cloud. The tool kit can be found at:	www.himss.org/cloud-compu ting-healthcare-toolkit
Wikipedia	https://en.wikipedia.org/wiki/ Cloud_computing
Amazon Cloud Services	https://aws.amazon.com/what-is -cloud-computing/
Google Cloud Services	https://cloud.google.com/
Microsoft Cloud Services	https://azure.microsoft.com/ en-us/
California Consumer Privacy Act (CCPA)	https://ccpa-info.com/

Resources

1. Final Version of NIST Cloud Computing Definition Published. *NIST,* October 25, 2011. Updated January 8, 2018. https://www.nist.gov/news-events/ne ws/2011/10/final-version-nist-cloud-computing-definition-published. Accessed January 24, 2020.
2. Rickter, Felix. Apple's App Store is Growing by 1,000+ Apps a Day. *Statista,* June 5, 2015. https://www.statista.com/chart/3530/app-store-growth/. Accessed January 24, 2020.
3. Press Release: Gartner Forecasts Worldwide Public Cloud Revenue to Grow 17.5 Percent in 2019. Gartner, April 2, 2019. https://www.gartner.com/en/new sroom/press-releases/2019-04-02-gartner-forecasts-worldwide-public-cloud-re venue-to-g. Accessed January 24, 2020.

Chapter 3

Cybersecurity Threats beyond EHR

Going beyond EHR would not be complete without a comprehensive look at new cybersecurity threats and the ways in which criminals are maliciously pursuing our EHR systems. News breaks daily with headlines about cybersecurity breaches across all industries, with the latest data showing substantial increases in attacks from across the globe. Figure 3.1 shows the amount of damage resulting from cybercrime over the past two decades.[1]

Healthcare organizations are not immune to the same threats facing other industries. However, the losses from exposure may exceed those of other business entities due to the sensitive nature of data and compliance laws and penalties. While cybersecurity in healthcare is improving, there is still lots of ground to cover in order to have adequate protection. Moreover, fighting cybercriminals is a "cat-and-mouse game" in that the would-be criminals are continually pursuing their targets to exploit the next vulnerability. The prospective victims are in perpetual defense mode, which means their efforts *MUST* be proactive – not merely responsive. The best practice is to deploy a mission to seek and destroy by actively patrolling for threats, much like a police department that operates a neighborhood watch program.

In addition to the data breach threats, cybersecurity in healthcare is also critical to patient safety. Attacks on systems storing patient information, medical devices and a hospital's information systems can have serious consequences. Disrupting the delivery of services is not only putting patients at risk for medical identity theft, it may also endanger the lives of individuals who have medical devices that rely on data to perform their vital functions.

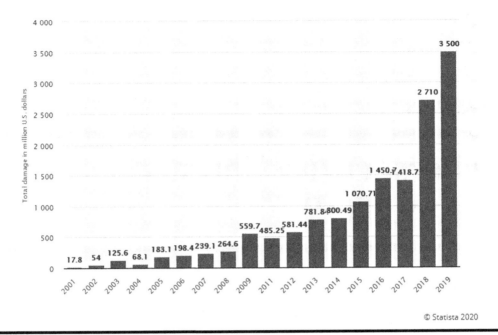

Figure 3.1   Amounts of monetary damage caused by reported cybercrime from 2001 to 2019 (in million U.S. dollars).

These disruptions are the same reasons why airlines prohibit the use of cell phones during take-offs and landings. (Note: Passengers are still not allowed to use their cellular connection to text on a plane, but since October 2013, the use of devices like iPhones and tablets is allowed on flights within the U.S., provided they are in airplane mode while taxiing and in the sky.)[2]

The Health Insurance Portability and Accountability Act (HIPAA) security rule requires that covered entities conduct a security risk analysis (SRA) of their healthcare organization.

In the following pages, we address the problem of cybersecurity breaches, sources of threats, the Chief Information Officer's (CIO) responsibilities, working with third-party vendors and conducting privacy and security risk analyses. The information will help your organization take proactive steps to gain ground in developing and maintaining a strong cybersecurity posture. There is much catching up to do.

Cybersecurity Breaches on the Rise

As evidenced by the steady rise in hacking and IT security incidents over recent years, many healthcare organizations have struggled to defend their networks. Today, healthcare IT departments must protect multiple connected medical and non-medical devices. Additionally, the number of Internet of things (IoT) devices integrated into the healthcare industry has exploded. (Chapter 12 addresses the topic of IoT.) Data are the new currency, and cybercriminals will stop at nothing to gain access to this valuable commodity. These offenders are developing more sophisticated methods and techniques to attack healthcare organizations and increase their chances of cashing in these data by holding them at ransom or selling them on the black market.

The 2019 HIMSS Cybersecurity Survey, available at www.himss.org/ himss-cybersecurity-survey, provides valuable insight into the information security experiences and practices of U.S. healthcare organizations that have been hacked and compromised. Over 160 U.S.-based health information security professionals were polled, and the findings reflect the following:

■ **A pattern of cybersecurity threats and experiences is discernable across U.S. healthcare organizations**. Significant security incidents are almost a universal experience in U.S. healthcare organizations with many of the events initiated by bad actors, leveraging e-mail to compromise the integrity of their targets.

■ **Many positive advances are occurring in healthcare cybersecurity practices**. Healthcare organizations appear to be allocating more of their information technology (IT) budgets to cybersecurity.

■ **Complacency with cybersecurity practices can put cybersecurity programs at risk**. Certain responses are not necessarily bad cybersecurity practices but may be an early warning signal about potential complacency seeping into the organization's information security practices.

■ **Notable cybersecurity gaps exist in critical areas of the healthcare ecosystem**. The lack of phishing tests in certain organizations and the prevalence of legacy systems raise serious concerns regarding the vulnerability of the healthcare ecosystem.

External Attacks

According to the Office for Civil Rights (OCR) at the U.S. Department of Health and Human Services (DHS), approximately 15% of healthcare providers reported a data breach due to a hacking of hospital IT systems in the past 24 months. The remainder of the victims were other types of healthcare

Table 3.1 Security incidents report

Recent Significant Security Incident	2019					2018
	Hospital	Non-Acute	Vendor	Other	Total	Total
Yes	82%	64%	68%	76%	74%	76%
No	14%	33%	30%	20%	22%	21%
Don't Know	4%	3%	3%	4%	4%	3%

organizations, such as physician practices, ambulatory surgical centers, mental health facilities, rehabilitation facilities and others. Further, approximately two-thirds of non-acute and vendor organizations reported experiencing a security incident in the past 12 months (see Table 3.1).[3]

Unfortunately, many healthcare organizations have been slow to respond to cybersecurity threats and lack various prevention tools. Hospitals also rely heavily on third-party vendors, where the attack can occur from within, as discussed below. Even though cybersecurity budgets have begun to increase, and healthcare entities are purchasing new cybersecurity technologies, they still struggle to thwart attacks and keep their networks secure proactively.

Insider Threats

Insider threats happen when the vulnerability originates within the organization and from a trusted source. These incidents are incredibly complicated to prevent for obvious reasons. A security incident does not mean there are bad actors on the inside; instead, there is an employee who has been compromised unknowingly. The infraction could be as simple as the employee using the same user ID and password they use for their social media accounts. When these accounts get compromised, the hacker knows that people commonly use the same passwords. Hence, they begin to target the individual to figure out where they work and what additional information can they gain and use to manipulate them into giving up their credentials. This technique is called social engineering, and it can be challenging to prevent because it relies on the poor judgment of the manipulated person with their private information. According to a recent Verizon Data Breach Investigation Report, 58% of healthcare PHI breaches are caused by insiders. The report went on to state that healthcare was the only industry where internal actors are the greatest threat.[4]

Healthcare data may be thought of as something that is just internally, but we share data with a wide variety of individuals to facilitate the coordination and delivery of care. This activity requires us to secure the data while ensuring access to those who need it, which adds a layer of complexity. Even with the increased transition to electronic health record (EHR) systems, paper records are causing data security problems, according to the Verizon study. Hardcopy documents were the assets most often involved in incidents involving error. Healthcare organizations, therefore, should consider instituting an effective risk management program that invests in comprehensive data breach detection measures. This program would include table-top exercises and the review of Internet of things (IoT) security as just a few of the prevention and detection requisites. Additionally, healthcare leaders must ensure that internal staff has adequate cybersecurity training and resources needed to ensure the appropriate precautions are taken to protect sensitive data from compromise by internal and external bad actors.

Social Engineering

The aim of "social engineering" is for the hacker to create a tactic that is personalized to the target. In some cases, they will even use emotion to throw off their victims. For example, they will search your Facebook page or public records to see if you had any recent deaths in the family. Then, they will send a fake e-mail or message claiming they have an asset or funds they are attempting to return to the deceased family member. The cyber-criminals will use anything imaginable, including deceased relatives, to trick their victims. Once the victims click on these links or sign up for whatever is being offered, they will used this as a backdoor channel to gain access. We saw a sharp rise in social engineering during the COVID-19 crisis when health systems sent their providers home to do telemedicine visits. The hackers started going after home networks, knowing physicians were seeing and treating patients from their home computers.

Hackers are exploiting other mediums, not just home networks. They are also attacking the telemedicine platforms. COVID-19 is fueling an uptick in ransomware attacks and giving cybercriminals an edge. Zoom, one of the more popular platforms for video conferencing, was recently attacked, as well.[5]

So, what can we do?

From an IT environmental perspective, if the home is being used to conduct official office work where PHI is involved, it MUST be treated as an extension of the office where the devices in use come under the same management controls. The IT staff must immediately implement the same policies and set up the same managed IT services as they would in any office. This is now a remote office.

Additional tips:

- Immediately, have all of your providers opt out of the people finder websites. These are creepy websites that aggregate personal information from thousands of sources and make it available to the public. These sites can supply details as specific as the type of car you drive and the names of your immediate family members. Hackers will use this information to conduct their social engineering operations. Opting out takes time, but by law, these websites must give you that option.
- Call a family meeting and tell EVERYONE to lock their Facebook accounts to the highest privacy settings, meaning only trusted people in their network can see their information.
- Explain social engineering to your kids. This lesson is something we need to be teaching regardless of whether you are using your home network as a remote office.
- For those working from home, turn off all your listening devices. You do not need Alexa eavesdropping on your virtual visits.
- Consider unplugging non-essential Internet of things (IoT) devices.
- (Note: The Internet of things (IoT) is a system of interrelated computing devices, mechanical and digital machines provided with unique identifiers (UIDs) and the ability to transfer data over a network without requiring human-to-human or human-to-computer interaction. See Chapter 12 for IoT information.)

The illustration in Figure 3.2 is a map that sequences cybersecurity theft.

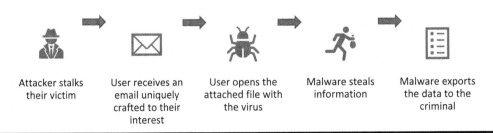

| Attacker stalks their victim | User receives an email uniquely crafted to their interest | User opens the attached file with the virus | Malware steals information | Malware exports the data to the criminal |

Figure 3.2 Pathway to cybersecurity theft.

Cybersecurity and Today's Healthcare Chief Information Officer

Among other compliance requirements, cybersecurity continues to be top-of-mind for healthcare chief information officers (CIOs), chief information security officers (CISOs), executives and management. Healthcare entities face the challenge of balancing the need to have easy access to information while keeping it tightly secure. As CIOs seek ways to achieve this balance, they are trying to move from a reactive to a *proactive* position in several key areas, including the considerations in Table 3.2.

Mere compliance with privacy, security and confidentiality regulations is no longer enough. Violating these regulations often results in tens or hundreds of thousands of dollars in fines, not to mention the potential destruction of an organization's information assets, an adverse patient outcome or negative publicity. CIOs must proactively secure and monitor their networks, applications systems and data while conducting periodic security audits.

As the number and complexity of IT systems, devices and users grow over time, forward-thinking CIOs are welcoming third-party advisors to conduct ongoing security audits, assessments and penetration tests. These advisors use human interaction with specialized automated tools to conduct and report on these security activities. The existence of and compliance with updated privacy and security policies are under closer scrutiny, along with employee behavior and habits in following these policies. Additionally, updated cybercrime and security education and training must be implemented on an ongoing basis.

CIOs are **expected** to develop and implement a cyber defense strategy to protect their healthcare organizations and patient information. Those CIOs who openly assess their vulnerabilities, prioritize their actions and continually monitor and manage their security risks are best positioned to help their organizations grow efficiently, effectively and safely.

Third-Party Vendors

If dealing with your own security threats was not a big enough challenge, you must also ensure all your business associate (BA) partners are compliant. A "business associate" is a person or entity, other than a member of the workforce of a covered entity, who performs functions or activities on behalf of, or provides certain services to, a covered entity that involves access

Table 3.2 Security Considerations

Security Area	Considerations
1. EHR system security	• EHR vendors have included various layers of security to protect unauthorized access to the EHR. CIOs must ensure that their EHR vendors and EHR system(s) security work in harmony with their network perimeter security to avoid negatively impacting an authorized user, preventing them from accessing the system or degrading EHR system performance. This collaboration should be assessed and verified each time there is a change or upgrade made to the EHR system or the network perimeter.
2. Network perimeter security	• Also known as a demilitarized zone (DMZ), perimeter security addresses the boundary between the private, locally managed and owned side of a network and the public and externally managed network, such as the Internet. The DMZ is one of the highest security risks that must be continually assessed, tested and addressed.
3. End-user authentication	• Users logging on to an organization's wired or wireless network to access protected health information continues to create challenges. This increased amount of network traffic takes advanced tools to monitor for unauthorized access. All log-in attempts must be monitored and acted upon accordingly. Some CIOs have implemented a single-sign-on (SSO) solution to control and resolve these issues. Whatever solution is deployed, organizations must test, document and resolve authentication issues continually.
4. User identity	• More organizations are implementing a virtual desktop infrastructure (VDI) in their EHR environments. It often becomes difficult to capture and audit user identities in these environments, which further raises security risks.
5. Internet of things ("IoT")	• We are seeing an exponential increase in the number of items (devices) becoming computer-based and linked to the Internet. IoT devices, such as biomedical, security cameras and HVAC systems, must be identified, continually monitored for security risks and managed.

by the business associate to protected health information. Many organizations mistakenly assume a signed business associate agreement (BAA) is enough to ensure that third-party vendors are compliant and responsible for their own breaches. Covered entities must ensure that they have a current HIPAA business associate agreement in place with each of their partners to maintain PHI security and overall HIPAA compliance. These partnerships are known as "business associate agreements."

While having a BAA is a critical first step, it is insufficient in and of itself. There are three common misconceptions about the BAA.

1. The third-party vendor or person doing work for the hospital/practice is not storing PHI data; therefore, they are not considered a BAA.

   False: If they have access to data, they qualify as a BA and must sign a BAA.

2. All third-party vendors use encryption and offer a privacy statement.

   False: They still have access to the data, and encryption is not always a 100% safeguard.

3. The vendor already has a BAA with the hospital and practice; therefore, any of their subcontractors or partners will be covered under the same BAA.

   False: ANY subcontractors working on behalf of a vendor will also require a BAA. The latest rules state that covered entities MUST ensure they obtain satisfactory assurances from their business associates, which includes their sub-contractors.

4. The vendor does not have to do a security risk analysis.

   False: Any vendor who is engaged with a covered entity must also perform a security risk analysis and should be required to produce a copy of their results.

Many security breaches happen because of third-party vendors using down-the-chain people who do not directly contract with the hospital/practice. In some cases, these are individuals from staffing agencies and/or who work as freelancers. They will usually be unaware of the policies or standards. They carry no insurance and would have no means of protecting anyone if they caused a breach, so there would be little to no recourse. Further, they may be outsourced to another country and not in the U.S. Therefore, here are several tips to reduce security threats when working with third-party vendors:

- All subcontractors must be preapproved. Under no circumstances can any vendor use subcontractors without prior permission.
- Vendors must disclose all existing subcontractors and require each to sign the BAA provided by the hospital/practice and present proof of insurance. If covered under the primary vendor's insurance policy, require evidence.
- All vendor contracts should require provisions about cybersecurity breaches. Specifically, the vendor must be responsible for their mistakes and the cost to remediate the issues.
- The BAA should have a breach notification requirement mandating the vendor to notify the hospital/practice of any incidents.
- There should be a data return policy and/or destruction requirement.
- System access should have a start and end date. Most systems today allow for setting an expiration date.
- Require the right to audit and inspect adherence to these policies at any time.
- Have vendors provide evidence of their security risk analysis, compliance certifications and proof of staff privacy training.
- Revisit policies and the BAA after each major upgrade, new release and version change as these events are when new contractors are often introduced.
- Consider adopting contract management software to help manage and track key dates and documents as these BAAs are updated annually.

Privacy and Security Risk Analysis

The Health Insurance Portability and Accountability Act (HIPAA) Security Rule requires that covered entities conduct an SRA of their healthcare organization. A risk analysis helps your organization meet all HIPAA-imposed compliance standards. These standards fall into three categories (see Figure 3.3).

A risk analysis also helps identify and detect areas where your organization's protected health information (PHI) could be at risk.

As noted above, the Final Omnibus Rule, which updated the HIPAA Security Rule and Breach Notification Rule of the HITECH Act, now requires

Technical
Monitoring Tools

Authentication

Access control

Audit Control

Integrity

Physical Safeguards
Access Control

Workstation Use

Workstation Security

Device and Media Control

Administrative
Policies and Procedures

Contingency Plans

Staff Education

Notices

BAA / SRA

Figure 3.3   HIPAA compliance standards categories.

the covered entity to ensure their business associates also follow these same policies, including conducting the SRA.[6]

The failure to conduct the SRA can be costly. Fines for non-compliance with HIPAA are much more severe when negligence can be shown. This is especially true when issues are known but dismissed as insignificant. The "Did Not Know" excuse is no longer acceptable as the HIPAA requirements have been known for a decade.

The OCR has the responsibility to guide regulated entities in conducting risk assessments. *Guidance on Risk Analysis Requirements under the HIPAA Security Rule* describes nine essential elements a risk assessment must incorporate, regardless of the risk analysis methodology employed.[7]

OCR published a nine-page PDF in July 2010, entitled "HHS/OCR Guidance on Risk Analysis Requirements under the HIPAA Security Rule." The guidance specifies nine essential requirements as follows:

1. **Scope of the analysis**. All ePHI that an organization creates, receives, maintains or transmits must be included in the risk analysis. (See 45 C.F.R. § 164.306(a).)
2. **Data collection**. The data on ePHI gathered using these methods must be documented. (See 45 C.F.R. §§ 164.308(a)(1)(ii)(A) and 164.316 (b)(1).)
3. **Identify and document potential threats and vulnerabilities**. Organizations must identify and document reasonably anticipated threats to ePHI. (See 45 C.F.R. §§ 164.306(a)(2), 164.308(a)(1)(ii)(A) and 164.316(b)(1)(ii).)
4. **Assess current security measures**. Organizations should assess and document the security measures an entity uses to safeguard ePHI. (See 45 C.F.R. §§ 164.306(b)(1), 164.308(a)(1)(ii)(A), and 164.316(b)(1).)
5. **Determine the likelihood of threat occurrence**. The Security Rule requires organizations to take into account the likelihood of potential risks to ePHI. (See 45 C.F.R. § 164.306(b)(2)(iv).)

6. **Determine the potential impact of threat occurrence**. The rule also requires consideration of the "criticality," or impact, of potential risks to the confidentiality, integrity and availability of ePHI. (See 45 C.F.R. § 164.306(b)(2)(iv).)

7. **Determine the level of risk**. The level of risk could be determined, for example, by analyzing the values assigned to the likelihood of threat occurrence and resulting impact of threat occurrence. (See 45 C.F.R. §§ 164.306(a)(2), 164.308(a)(1)(ii)(A), and 164.316(b)(1).) The risk calculation process is taken from NIST 800-30.

8. **Finalize documentation**. The Security Rule requires the risk analysis to be documented but does not require a specific format. (See 45 C.F.R. § 164.316(b)(1).)

9. **Periodic review and updates to the risk analysis**. The risk analysis process should be ongoing. In order for an entity to update and document its security measures "as needed," which the rule requires, it should conduct continuous risk analysis to identify when updates are needed. (45 C.F.R. §§ 164.306(e) and 164.316(b)(2)(iii).)

Penalties

HIPAA was established in 1996, with an annual cap of $25,000 for all violations of an identical provision. Over the last two decades, only a few revisions have been made to the Civil Monetary Penalties (CMP) limits.

On April 26, 2019, the OCR announced a new structure for penalties. As a result of this change, the financial risks of HIPAA breach violations for covered entities that can demonstrate updated security risk management plans, policies and procedures for sensitive patient data were significantly reduced. Figure 3.4 and Table 3.3 illustrate the adjustments.

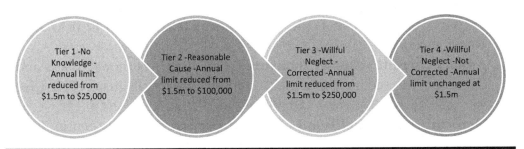

Figure 3.4   Key changes in HIPAA/HITECH CMP annual limits.

Table 3.3   2009 Annual Limits (HITECH)

Capacity	Minimum Penalty/ Violation	Maximum Penalty/ Violation	Annual Limit
Tier 1 – no knowledge	$100	$50,000	$1,500,000
Tier 2 – reasonable cause	$1,000	$50,000	$1,500,000
Tier 3 – willful neglect	$10,000	$50,000	$1,500,000
Tier 4 – willful neglect	$50,000	$50,000	$1,500,000

Completing the Security Risk Analysis

According to www.HealthIT.Gov, here are the "Top 10 Myths of Security Risk Analysis."[8]

1. **The security risk analysis is optional for small providers.**

   False: All providers who are "covered entities" under HIPAA are required to perform a risk analysis. In addition, all providers who want to receive EHR incentive payments must conduct a risk analysis.

2. **Simply installing a certified EHR fulfills the security risk analysis MU requirement.**

   False: Even with a certified EHR, you must perform a full security risk analysis. Security requirements address all electronic protected health information you maintain, not just what is in your EHR.

3. **My EHR vendor took care of everything I need to do about privacy and security.**

   False: Your EHR vendor may be able to provide information, assistance and training on the privacy and security aspects of the EHR product. However, EHR vendors are not responsible for making their products compliant with HIPAA Privacy and Security Rules. It is solely your responsibility to have a complete risk analysis conducted.

4. **I have to outsource the security risk analysis.**

   False: It is possible for small practices to do risk analysis themselves using self-help tools. However, doing a thorough and professional risk analysis that will stand up to a compliance review will require expert knowledge that could be obtained through the services of an experienced outside professional.

5. **A checklist will suffice for the risk analysis requirement.**

   False: Checklists can be useful tools, especially when starting a risk analysis, but they fall short of performing a systematic security risk analysis or documenting that one has been performed.

6. **There is a specific risk analysis method that I must follow.**

   False: A risk analysis can be performed in countless ways. The OCR has issued "Guidance on Risk Analysis Requirements of the Security Rule" available at www.hhs.gov/hipaa/for-professionals /security/guidance/guidance-risk-analysis/index.html. This guidance assists organizations in identifying and implementing the most effective and appropriate safeguards to secure e-PHI.

7. **My security risk analysis only needs to look at my EHR.**

   False: Review all electronic devices that store, capture or modify electronic protected health information. Include your EHR hardware and software and devices that can access your EHR data (e.g., your tablet computer, your practice manager's mobile phone). Remember that copiers also store data. Please see the "U.S. Department of Health and Human Services (HHS) Guidance on Telehealth Remote Communications" at www.hhs.gov/about/ne ws/2020/03/20/ocr-issues-guidance-on-telehealth-remote-commu nications-following-its-notification-of-enforcement-discretion.html.

8. **I only need to do a risk analysis once.**

   False: To comply with HIPAA, you must continue to review, correct or modify and update security protections. For more on reassessing your security practices, please see "Reassessing Your Security Practices in a Health IT Environment" at www.healthit.gov/resource /reassessing-your-security-practices-health-it-environment-guide-small-health-care.

9. **Before I attest for an EHR incentive program, I must fully mitigate all risks.**

   False: The EHR incentive program requires correcting any deficiencies (identified during the risk analysis) during the reporting period, as part of its risk management process.

10. **Each year, I will have to completely redo my security risk analysis.**

    False: Perform the full security risk analysis as you adopt an EHR. Each year or when changes to your practice or electronic systems occur, review and update the prior analysis for changes in risks. Under the Meaningful Use programs, reviews are required for each EHR reporting period. For EPs, the EHR reporting period will be 90 days or a full calendar year, depending on the EP's year of participation in the program.

In addition to the myths listed above, there needs to be a clear understanding of the difference between a security risk assessment and a security risk analysis.

- **High level = security risk assessment**: A judgment about something based on an understanding of the situation; a method of evaluating performance. This would be similar to a gap analysis.
- **Detailed analysis = security risk analysis**: Risk analysis is the assessment of the risks and vulnerabilities that could negatively impact the confidentiality, integrity and availability of the electronic protected health information (e-PHI) held by a covered entity, and the likelihood of occurrence. The risk analysis may include taking inventory of all systems and applications that are used to access and house data and classifying them by level of risk. A thorough and accurate risk analysis would consider all relevant losses that would be expected if the security measures were not in place, including loss or damage of data, corrupted data systems and anticipated ramifications of such losses or damage.

Considering how security risk and policies continue to evolve, we recommend following many of the official sites set up by CMS and the OCR that will supply the latest information. In most cases, these sites will provide

Table 3.4   Official Security Resource Sites

Resources	Links
Security Risk Analysis Tip Sheet	www.cms.gov/Regulations-and-Guidance/Legislation/EHRIncentivePrograms/Downloads/2016_SecurityRiskAnalysis.pdf
Security Risk Assessment Tool	www.healthit.gov/topic/privacy-security-and-hipaa/security-risk-assessment-tool
HIPAA Basics	www.healthit.gov/topic/privacy-security-and-hipaa/hipaa-basics
Privacy and Security Tools	www.healthit.gov/topic/privacy-security-and-hipaa/privacy-security-resources-tools
Security Risk Guidance	www.hhs.gov/hipaa/for-professionals/security/guidance/guidance-risk-analysis/index.html
How to Conduct a Security Risk Analysis	www.ama-assn.org/sites/ama-assn.org/files/corp/media-browser/public/ps2/tcpi-webinar-security-risk-analysis.pdf

simple-to-follow tip-sheets, data collection tools and sample reports. Table 3.4 is a list of "official" helpful websites.

Organizations that maintain thorough and well-documented HIPAA compliance and risk management programs reduce their risk of financial exposure to civil monetary penalties from HHS/OCR. Preserving the proper privacy and security documentation necessary to satisfy compliance with key HIPAA security rules is critical. This also includes conducting an SRA to help covered entities avoid the fourth and highest-level of liability for "willful neglect – not corrected." The SRA should occur at least annually and include an assessment of the covered entity's technology infrastructure and information security policies and procedures. The SRA should consist of a remediation plan to outline the actions that will be undertaken to address any weaknesses in the organization's security program.

Risk analysis and risk management tools can be effective resources in assessing and managing any gaps identified through the SRA process. Risk analysis tools can provide a method of documenting each recognized risk event or vulnerability point in the organization, including those with business associates. They also serve as a repository of your organization's security remediation efforts and can be evidence in the event that the covered entity is subject to an audit from the OCR. This detailed documentation confirms that a covered entity has an effective risk management program in place and may help to prevent the "not corrected" status associated with the $1.5 million annual limit.

Also, OCR stated that it will be actively auditing organizations that **do not** report any breaches. Therefore, covered entities with the most correct security risk analysis and comprehensive breach detection program will have a reduced likelihood of the imposition of fines and penalties because of a security audit or breach.

Summary

The findings of the 2019 HIMSS Cybersecurity Survey suggest that healthcare organizations' cybersecurity initiatives are moving in the right direction with some degree of uniformity. However, we still have a long way to go in comparison to other industries. While the progress is positive, budgets allocated to cybersecurity are still inadequate to deal with all the emerging cybersecurity threats that most healthcare organizations face. Moreover, the lack of knowledgeable cybersecurity personnel also continues as a detriment to progress.

Legacy systems and the lack of staff awareness continue to present a problem in need of innovative approaches. Overall, healthcare organizations are moving in the right direction, but bad actors continue to stay one step ahead of the game.

Resources

1. Amount of Monetary Damage Caused by Reported Cyber Crime to the IC3 from 2001 to 2019. *Statista.com*, March 27, 2020. https://www.statista.com/stati stics/267132/total-damage-caused-by-by-cyber-crime-in-the-us/. Accessed May 4, 2020.
2. Cheslaw, Louis, Brady, Paul. Can you Text on a Plane? A Guide to Inflight Phone Use. *Conde Nast Traveler*, July 22, 2019. https://www.cntraveler.com/sto ries/2014-06-16/everything-you-need-to-know-about-using-a-cell-phone-on-a-plane. Accessed April 14, 2020.
3. HIMSS. 2019 HIMSS Cybersecurity Survey. https://www.himss.org/sites/hi mssorg/files/u132196/2019_HIMSS_Cybersecurity_Survey_Final_Report.pdf. Accessed April 14, 2019.
4. Snell, Elizabeth. 58% of Healthcare PHI Data Breaches Caused by Insiders. *Health IT Security*. Accessed April 15, 2019. https://healthitsecurity.com/news/ 58-of-healthcare-phi-data-breaches-caused-by-insiders.

5. Tiziana, Celine. Video Calling Service Zoom Sued by Own Stakeholder for Not Revealing Privacy, Security Breach. *Tech Times*, April 8, 2020. https://ww w.techtimes.com/articles/248675/20200408/video-calling-service-zoom-sued-by -own-stakeholder-for-not-revealing-privacy-security-breach.htm. Accessed May 4, 2020.
6. Omnibus HIPAA Rulemaking. https://www.hhs.gov/hipaa/for-professionals/ privacy/laws-regulations/combined-regulation-text/omnibus-hipaa-rulemaking/ index.html. Accessed May 4, 2020.
7. DHS. Guidance on Risk Analysis Requirements Under the HIPAA Security Rule. July 14, 2010. Accessed April 16, 2019. https://www.hhs.gov/sites/default/ files/ocr/privacy/hipaa/administrative/securityrule/rafinalguidancepdf.pdf.
8. Health IT.gov. Top 10 Myths of Security Risk Analysis. https://www.healthit .gov/topic/privacy-security-and-hipaa/top-10-myths-security-risk-analysis. Accessed May 5, 2020.

Chapter 4

Health Information Technology Compliance

Compliance in the realm of health information technology (HIT) will be challenging to cover in a single chapter of a book. This broad topic and the levels of detail required for staying compliant, as well as the penalties for dereliction of duties, call for a thorough examination in order to stay abreast of the everchanging landscape of IT compliance in healthcare.

It has been over ten years since the HITECH Act rollout, which heightened the requirements for the adoption of technology in healthcare environments. These additional constraints have led to more resources being necessary to ensure organizations stay compliant to avoid penalties associated with these demands. While many of the fundamental requirements have not varied, the amount of oversight of organizations' processes and protocols necessary to ensure staff at all levels have compliant workflows embedded into daily operations and tasks has increased. This chapter will review the evolution of compliance in the field of healthcare technology and what risks these requirements were introduced to thwart through the principle of cybersecurity. We will also look at the human capital necessary to maintain policies to achieve regulatory compliance.

Compliance – Then to Now

The matter of compliance in its relationship to the technology used in healthcare has journeyed through various stages, especially with incentive programs. The measures for achieving compliance have developed, as well.

Various Stages of Program Incentives

The Health Information Technology for Economic and Clinical Health (HITECH) Act is the technology compliance component of the American Recovery and Reinvestment Act of 2009 (ARRA). ARRA included several channels of investment into the U.S. economy through a stimulus package to provide improvements to various segments of infrastructure and technologies. The target of the HITECH Act was to address the anticipated expansion of patient data that would be contained in electronic formats. This growth was easily predictable due to the incentive programs within the stimulus bill to pay physicians and healthcare organizations for the adoption of electronic health records.

Within the incentive program outlined in the HITECH Act of 2009, providers were expected to demonstrate Meaningful Use (MU) of certified electronic health records (EHR). By meeting the requirements and attesting to the achievement of clinical measures, providers were given monetary incentives by CMS. While these incentives were initially offered until 2015, many of the programs experienced delays, and some stages were not officially completed until 2018. The adoption of office-based physician EHRs across the country more than doubled between 2008 and 2017 due to these incentives, as Figure 4.1 illustrates. These types of statistics were evidence that the

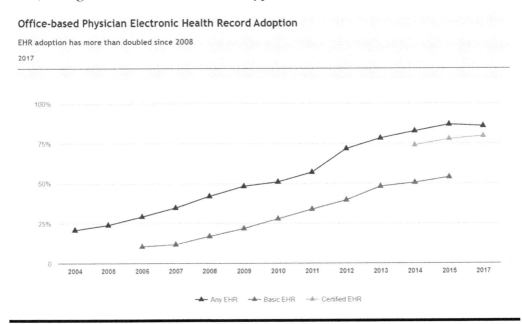

Office-based Physician Electronic Health Record Adoption

EHR adoption has more than doubled since 2008

Figure 4.1   Office-based physician electronic health record adoption. Source: https://dashboard.healthit.gov/quickstats/pages/physician-ehr-adoption-trends.php.

government had to establish governance over the method that an industry, new to the adoption of technology at the point of care, would need in order to ensure privacy and security for their new inheritance of data wealth.

Now, the fine print of the incentive program also outlined the expansion of the scope of privacy and security contained within the HIPAA Act of 1996. Whether or not an organization attested to the MU programs, the HITECH Act required adherence to existing HIPAA rules. As an example, covered entities that share patient information are required to obtain business associate agreements (BAA) from their business associates. With the adoption of electronic health records, organizations have found the need to establish outside relationships to manage patient data and new systems. This once-overlooked policy has become the root of several data breaches, which have led to substantial penalties and fines for multiple healthcare organizations.

Meaningful Use audits were an early sign that the Centers for Medicare and Medicaid Services (CMS) wanted to ensure that providers who attested to meeting their program guidelines were sincere in doing so. Many of the audits were completed after providers received their incentive payment; other audits were done before. CMS outsourced the auditing task to the certified public accountant firm Figliozzi and Company. In some cases, the firm would appear onsite to observe the demonstration of the EMR system used to attest to the CMS program. In most cases, however, a letter was sent to the contact e-mail address on file requesting documentation (reports extracted) from the certified EMR, proving the accuracy of the figures reported. These auditing steps placed the responsibility on the provider/staff to use workflows to capture the required data used for Meaningful Use. However, the onus for the technology used to claim an EMR was certified was placed on the software companies' ability to produce accurate reports. These audits led to fines levied on several EMR vendors, as well as some losing their accreditation, which lead to the shrinking of the EMR vendor market.

How to Achieve Regulatory Compliance

After doubling the number of providers using EMRs, the variety, volume and rate of personal clinical data transmitted between healthcare organizations have grown significantly. This growth has placed more emphasis on compliance, with privacy and security regulations for all healthcare organizations.

Unlike the MU attestation, where the use of a certified system was being examined, the current compliance obligations lie in organizations' ability to avert risk. While HIPAA outlines safeguards to protect against e-PHI, today's advanced healthcare systems must take a holistic approach to protecting their patient's data. Table 4.1 summarizes the fundamental safeguards that the HIPAA guidelines provide. The full text is available at www.hhs.gov/hip aa/for-professionals/security/laws-regulations/index.html.

Staying compliant in the new era of technologically advanced healthcare systems does not start and end at the IT department. Every employee has the responsibility to adhere to standards and policies outlined by their compliance department. Depending on the organization's size, the duty for oversight and development of adherence to compliance may fall on a single individual or a team of staff members (Figure 4.2).

The Office of Health and Human Services (HHS) published a notice on January 31, 2005, to outline supplemental guidance for hospitals. The full document is available as the Federal Register/Vol. 70, No. 19/Monday, January 31, 2005/Notices, at https://oig.hhs.gov/fraud/docs/complianceguid ance/012705HospSupplementalGuidance.pdf. Table 4.2 illustrates these guidance points.

As we take a deeper look into healthcare IT and the compliance requirements, we will focus on the structure of a typical healthcare system's IT compliance team. Regardless of size, the goal of staying compliant is to safeguard patients; thus, smaller organizations can assess their compliance team and scale their team to their needs. Healthcare compliance teams are not always 100% internal to the healthcare organization. The technology standards and security protocols that serve as the foundation of all technology communications and infrastructure are established by the International Organization for Standardization (ISO). This organization develops the "documents that provide requirements, specifications, guidelines or characteristics that can be used consistently to ensure that materials, products, processes, and services are fit for their purpose" within the technology realm of healthcare devices and applications.[1] These are the standards that organizations' (internal and/or external) security analysts and operations teams use to implement best practices relative to securing the data that are transferred from system to system.

Security consultants serve as subject-matter experts who specialize in strategies for implementing technical, administrative and physical safeguards needed for strong compliance policies. IT teams and support personnel are also critical components of the overall compliance team. These groups work hand in hand with end-users to support the data analytics, workflows and

Table 4.1   Summary of Safeguards of the HIPAA Security Rule

Administrative safeguards	Security management process. As explained in the previous section, a covered entity must identify and analyze potential risks to e-PHI, and it must implement security measures that reduce risks and vulnerabilities to a reasonable and appropriate level. Security personnel. A covered entity must designate a security official who is responsible for developing and implementing its security policies and procedures. Information access management. Consistent with the privacy rule standard limiting uses and disclosures of PHI to the "minimum necessary," the security rule requires a covered entity to implement policies and procedures for authorizing access to e-PHI only when such access is appropriate based on the user or recipient's role (role-based access). Workforce training and management. A covered entity must provide for the appropriate authorization and supervision of workforce members who work with e-PHI. A covered entity must train all workforce members regarding its security policies and procedures and must have and apply appropriate sanctions against workforce members who violate its policies and procedures. Evaluation. A covered entity must perform a periodic assessment of how well its security policies and procedures meet the requirements of the security rule.
Physical safeguards	Facility access and control. A covered entity must limit physical access to its facilities while ensuring that authorized access is allowed. Workstation and device security. A covered entity must implement policies and procedures to specify the proper use of and access to workstations and electronic media. A covered entity also must have in place policies and procedures regarding the transfer, removal, disposal and re-use of electronic media to ensure appropriate protection of electronic protected health information (e-PHI).
Technical safeguards	Access control. A covered entity must implement technical policies and procedures that allow only authorized persons to access electronic protected health information (e-PHI). Audit controls. A covered entity must implement hardware, software, and/or procedural mechanisms to record and examine access and other activity in information systems that contain or use e-PHI. Integrity controls. A covered entity must implement policies and procedures to ensure that e-PHI is not improperly altered or destroyed. Electronic measures must be put in place to confirm that e-PHI has not been improperly altered or destroyed. Transmission security. A covered entity must implement technical security measures that guard against unauthorized access to e-PHI that is being transmitted over an electronic network.

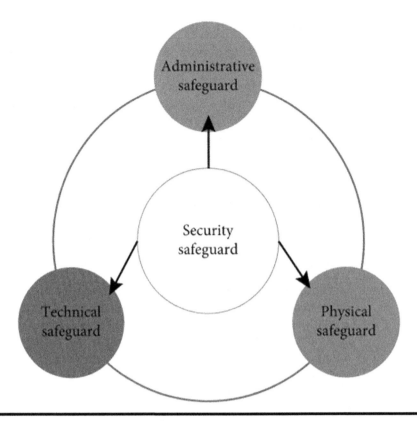

Figure 4.2   Illustrates the circle of responsibility for safeguards in the scope of the organization. Source: https://static-01.hindawi.com/articles/wcmc/volume-2019/1927 495/figures/1927495.fig.002.svgz

technical support needed to guard patient data. A complete compliance team also requires legal oversight from an attorney who understands the regulatory requirements and penalties and will serve as a subsequent advisor to the organization. The chief information officer (CIO) is the executive leader who bears the responsibility of oversight and administration of IT's responsibilities for security. This accountability is to executive stakeholders, the board of directors and other trading partners within the community that the healthcare system supports. Figure 4.3 illustrates the typical healthcare compliance team, as presented by TrueNorth HITG, Inc.[2]

Collectively, this team of experts, in conjunction with a compliance officer, forms the resources necessary to build an effective healthcare compliance program by:

■ Establishing a compliance committee
■ Developing compliance-based standard operating procedures (living document)

Table 4.2 Summary of Guidance Points Issued by HHS

Factors of Compliance	*Resources*	*Elements*
Designation of a compliance officer and compliance committee.	Compliance officer Compliance committee	Does the compliance department have a clear, well-crafted mission? Is the compliance department properly organized? Does the compliance department have sufficient resources (staff and budget), training, authority and autonomy to carry out its mission? Is the relationship between the compliance function and the general counsel function appropriate to achieve the purpose of each? Is there an active compliance committee comprised of trained representatives of each of the relevant functional departments as well as senior management? Does the compliance officer make regular reports to the board of directors and other hospital management concerning different aspects of the hospital's compliance program?
Development of compliance policies and procedures, including standards of conduct.	Compliance-based standard operating procedures (living document)	Are policies and procedures clearly written, relevant to day-to-day responsibilities, readily available to those who need them and re-evaluated on a regular basis? Does the hospital monitor staff compliance with internal policies and procedures? Have the standards of conduct been distributed to all directors, officers, managers, employees, contractors and medical and clinical staff members? Has the hospital developed a risk assessment tool, which is re-evaluated on a regular basis, to assess and identify weaknesses and risks in operations? Does the risk assessment tool include an evaluation of federal healthcare program requirements?

(Continued)

Table 4.2 (Continued)   Summary of Guidance Points Issued by HHS

Factors of Compliance	Resources	Elements
Developing open lines of communication.	Public-facing reporting tool with anonymous reporting mechanisms	Has the hospital fostered an organizational culture that encourages open communication, without fear of retaliation? Has the hospital established an anonymous hotline or another similar mechanism so that staff, contractors, patients, visitors and medical and clinical staff members can report potential compliance issues? How well is the hotline publicized; how many and what types of calls are received; are calls logged and traced (to establish possible patterns); and is the caller informed of the hospital's actions? Are all instances of potential fraud and abuse investigated? Are the results of internal investigations shared with the hospital governing body and relevant departments on a regular basis? Is the governing body actively engaged in pursuing appropriate remedies to institutional or recurring problems?
Appropriate training and education.	Regularly scheduled training and education content	Does the hospital provide qualified trainers to conduct annual compliance training for its staff, including both general and specific training pertinent to the staff's responsibilities? Has the hospital evaluated the content of its training and education program on an annual basis and determined that the subject content is appropriate and sufficient to cover the range of issues confronting its employees? Has the hospital kept up to date with any changes in federal healthcare program requirements and adapted its education and training program accordingly? Has the hospital formulated the content of its education and training program to consider results from its audits and investigations? Does the hospital seek feedback after each session to identify shortcomings in the training program, and does it administer post-training testing to ensure attendees understand and retain the subject matter delivered?

(Continued)

Table 4.2 (Continued)   Summary of Guidance Points Issued by HHS

Factors of Compliance	Resources	Elements
Internal monitoring and auditing.	Auditing tools	Is the audit plan re-evaluated annually, and does it address the proper areas of concern, considering, for example, findings from previous years' audits, risk areas identified as part of the annual risk assessment and high-volume services? Does the audit plan include an assessment of billing systems, in addition to claims accuracy, to identify the root cause of billing errors? Is the role of the auditors clearly established, and are coded and audit personnel independent and qualified, with the requisite certifications? Is the audit department available to conduct unscheduled reviews? Has the hospital evaluated the error rates identified in the annual audits? Does the audit include a review of all billing documentation, including clinical documentation, in support of the claim?
Response to detected deficiencies.	Mitigation plan and corrective action plans	Has the hospital created a response team, consisting of representatives from the compliance, audit and any other relevant functional areas, which may be able to evaluate any detected deficiencies quickly? Are all matters thoroughly and promptly investigated? Are corrective action plans developed that consider the root causes of each potential violation? Are periodic reviews of problem areas conducted to verify that the corrective action that was implemented successfully eliminated existing deficiencies? When a detected deficiency results in an identified overpayment to the hospital, are overpayments promptly reported and repaid to the FI? If a matter results in a probable violation of law, does the hospital promptly disclose the matter to the appropriate law enforcement agency?

(Continued)

Table 4.2 (Continued)   Summary of Guidance Points Issued by HHS

Factors of Compliance	Resources	Elements
Enforcement of disciplinary standards.	Standards for disciplinary actions	Are disciplinary standards well-publicized and readily available to all hospital personnel? Are disciplinary standards enforced consistently across the organization? Is each instance involving the enforcement of disciplinary standards documented thoroughly? Are employees, contractors and medical and clinical staff members checked routinely against government sanctions lists, including the OIG's List of Excluded Individuals/Entities and the General Services Administration's Excluded Parties Listing System?

Figure 4.3   Healthcare compliance team – best practice.

- Implementing public-facing reporting tools with anonymous reporting mechanisms
- Holding regularly scheduled training sessions with educational content
- Utilizing auditing tools
- Creating and maintaining mitigation plans and corrective action plans
- Cultivating standards for disciplinary actions

Summary

The HIPAA Act of 1996 was the foundation for establishing the privacy of patient information, as healthcare providers exchanged data for the treatment and payment of patient services. The HITECH Act of 2009 further increased the adherence to these fundamental protocols, as the large-scale adoption of technology through a stimulus package was expected to put patient data at higher risk. While data breaches are one mechanism for unauthorized access to patient data, modern health IT compliance teams must look past criminal threats, to also examine internal factors that may lead to unauthorized access to patient data. Developing standards and policies, conducting training and education, monitoring and auditing behaviors and enforcing disciplinary actions are major pillars for establishing the groundwork for protecting patient data and adhering to regulatory compliance.

Resources

1. Standards. ISO standards are internationally agreed upon by experts. www.iso. org/standards.html. Accessed March 30, 2020.
2. TrueNorth. Addressing the top IT healthcare compliance issues. www.trueno rthitg.com/addressing-top-healthcare-compliance-issues/. Accessed March 30, 2020.

Chapter 5

Using Artificial Intelligence in Healthcare

The adoption of artificial intelligence (AI) in healthcare is rising and delivering positive signs in assisting and solving a variety of problems for patients, providers and hospitals. *Forbes* Magazine reports a 14× increase in AI start-ups since 2000. With investment in the industry up six-fold, topping out at over $3 billion, spending on AI is likely to surpass all the outlays on EHRs combined. This chapter explores the current uses of AI, e.g., listening devices and Web applications, facial recognition and its use in the exam room, and ethical questions that arise from the use of AI in healthcare. Lastly, we consider how to establish a strategy for implementing AI in your own practice or hospital.

What Is Artificial Intelligence?

First, let's define artificial intelligence.

- The essential requirement of AI is intelligence, defined as the ability to acquire and apply knowledge and skills. It is the capacity to interact (speech, vision, motion, manipulation), reason, learn, adapt and think abstractly, as measured by objective criteria, such as test taking. Also, the AI must be capable of adapting to the outcomes or variables on its own.
- The term *artificial intelligence* is an umbrella term for machines capable of perception, logic and learning. Today, there are two types of AI:

— **Machine learning** is a form of AI that employs algorithms capable of learning from data to make predictions or decisions; as the machine's exposure to data increases, the performance capabilities are improved. In some cases, this may be a simple "if, and, do what" programming logic. For example, the "if-then statement" is set as the most basic of all the programing controls. It tells your program to execute a certain code only if a statement is true. For example, the heart monitor will send an alert **if** blood pressure drops below a certain threshold, but only **if** the program detects that the monitor is connected to a patient. An example of the program language could look like the following

- Alert Monitor Alarm () {
  - ■ // the "if" clause: *blood pressure dropping*
  - ■ if (connected to patient){
  - ■ // the "then" clause: *sound the alarm*

    A single AI program could have millions of IF-AND-DO-WHAT programing lines of code/scripts for making split-second decisions like how the human brain might work. For example, if you see a person running toward you, your reaction will vary considerably depending on data already stored in your brain. Do you know the person? Do they look excited to see you? Are they running up to you to give you a hug? **If** all are true, the **do what** outcome would likely be to stay calm. If the person running toward you looks unfamiliar, angry and is carrying a knife, the **do what** outcome is to RUN!!!! Should such an event occur, the brain (or AI) quickly responds and adapts based on the incoming data. (See Figure 5.1 for an example of machine learning logic.)

— **Deep Learning AI** is also based on the IF-AND-DO-WHAT programing concept but will act more like the human brain and adjust behavior based on prior outcomes. Using the same example of a person running toward you, the brain will record a massive amount of data from that event (e.g., location, time, images, facial recognition, etc.), then use this stored information to make better decisions in the future, such as avoiding dark alleys at 2:00 AM. Deep learning uses many-layered neural networks (computer systems based on the human brain and nervous system) to build algorithms that find the most efficient way to perform a task based on vast sets of data. Deep learning will typically improve over time by adding all

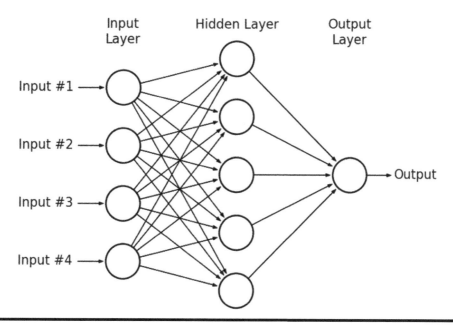

Figure 5.1   A hypothetical example of multilayer perceptron network.

past outcomes to the logic for future decisions. (See Figure 5.2.) One major limitation of the deep learning method is the inability to apply a conscience to decision-making. A major concern with the deep learning method is the possibility for bias and prejudice to seep into the algorithms. Bias in AI happens when the data used are unrepresentative of reality, or reflect the existing prejudices of the developer/programmer. An example of this was recently seen in AI software used to help judges in sentencing criminals based on the probability of the person being a repeat offender. Although AI is becoming better every day, the algorithms we see every day still have a long way to go before being safely applied to the criminal justice system.

While we do not foresee AI replacing all humans, the study of the ethics and risks of machine involvement in patient care, compared to traditional methods, has yet to catch up to the technology. More concerning is the overall impact on our society and the shifts in inequalities that AI is expected to cause. Specifically, AI is expected to eliminate 40% of all repetitive jobs over the next 20 years. Examples include call centers, patient check-in, registration, triage, collections, accounts receivable (AR) follow-up and campus delivery services. In March of 2019, UPS launched a new service using drones to transport blood and other medical supplies between the various buildings at the WakeMed Health and Hospitals medical campus in Raleigh,

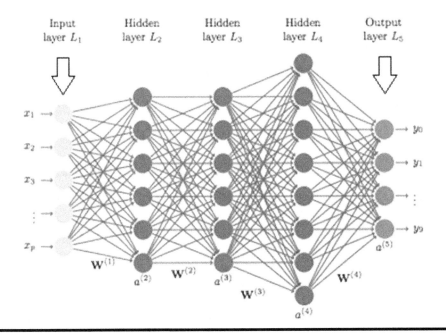

Figure 5.2   An illustration of a deep learning neural network.Source: www.resear chgate.net/figure/A-hypothetical-example-of-Multilayer-Perceptron-Network_fig4_3 03875065.

North Carolina.[1] The speed at which the drones delivered the samples was significantly faster compared to humans, which in this case could mean the difference between life and death. While this use of AI is a positive factor, the initiative instantly eliminated several courier jobs on campus. A few drone developer jobs were created, but the number of jobs eliminated compared to jobs created was far greater. However, expanded technology in any industry can be expected to create similar repercussions. This matter should not be seen as a deterrent from continuing the use of AI in the healthcare industry, as the benefits and capabilities of the technology are just beginning to surface. The possibility of eliminating jobs is always a by-product of innovation and should never be a justification for the status quo. For example, take a look at what Uber has done to the taxicab industry.

Listening Devices and Web Apps

As we investigate the future of AI, consider this scenario:

> While your physician is treating you, an AI listening device in
> the exam room makes thousands of calculations and predictions

based on the conversation it picks up between you and the physician. After the exam, the AI device may support the physician's decision-making and/or trigger additional action items, such as ordering the test the physician discussed with you. The AI may also warn the physician of a drug-to-drug interaction, because the AI device already knows what you have purchased over the counter, though you have forgotten to mention it to your physician. Did you know fish oil can be an anti-clotting agent and may negatively affect some treatment plans? Further, the AI already knows you just booked a trip to South America, so it generates a reminder for travel shots. The possibilities are endless.

Google reports that it already has access to 70% of our credit card transactions.[3] Therefore, the AI listening device in the exam room (provided by Google or Amazon) can be linked to the Google database of prior transactions, allowing the real-time conversation with the provider to be reconciled with other key data elements that impact your care. Does this feel a little creepy to you? Are you a bit nervous about data being gathered? Does it make you feel more confident knowing there is a second set of ears, albeit electronic ears, that is helping with decisions? What about all the genetic testing activities that are frequently and widely advertised? What if these data are combined with AI software to achieve a better understanding of past medical history from little-known relatives? The truth is this scenario is already happening all around us.

AI based on crowdsourcing data and/or accessing databases is constantly being utilized all around us. Most everyone has used GPS apps such as Google Maps or Waze. Have you ever seen the apps make real-time suggestions, such as offering new routes based on a set of circumstances like road construction or a traffic jam? Do you ever notice how Facebook and other social media apps seem to know your hobbies, travel preferences and even political affiliations and will make recommendations based on these preferences? Have you seen an ad pop up in your news feed after visiting a new place or restaurant even though you did not disclose your location? Many data collection agencies sell our data, and we often unknowingly release our data on many of the social media and Web-based platforms we regularly visit, such as Facebook, Twitter, Google and Amazon. These companies can see many of the pages you and others are visiting by using hidden tracking technologies, allowing them to tailor their ads accordingly. Another concern that arises is the potential for companies to eavesdrop on phone conversations. While tech companies deny that our phones are listening, devices like Amazon Echo, Alexa and Google Home are becoming increasingly popular. These devices do listen, albeit with the consent of the device's owner. We relinquish a lot of data in exchange for these technology benefits, and we unknowingly consent to giving up these data when we agree to use third-party apps or social medical platforms. Most people never read the lengthy, fine-print user agreements for these platforms, so we unknowingly agree to these terms, which often include stipulations for data collection. Despite a recent increase in public awareness concerning consumer rights and privacy, platform developers stand behind the notion that the use of their applications is a choice we make as consumers. Thus, as a user, we must accept their agreements to access their software.

What happens when these devices start making their way into exam rooms? Your place of work? In a private area? It is one thing for a consumer to invite an *always-listening* artificial intelligence device into their home knowingly, but should we have a right to know when we are being recorded? Under the wire-tap laws, most states prohibit one-party recording, but many companies get around this by having people waive their rights, or they might place a notice of advisement. For example, have you ever heard the statement, "This call may be recorded or monitored for educational purposes?" There is your notice of advisement. Some businesses will post signs letting you know the area is under video surveillance, which may have integrated facial recognition, which opens another world of AI possibilities.

Facial Recognition AI in Healthcare

Another form of AI is facial recognition. Some hospitals are using AI to detect pain or discomfort in patients' facial expressions, or to identify emotions such as stress, depression or anger in a person's voice. This technology is beneficial for nurse lines or suicide crisis centers, but it can also allow an entity to know personal information about each consumer who walks through the door so they can tailor how they interact with you. Some retailers use it to prevent theft by uploading pictures of known shoplifters, and restaurants can identify a big tipper/spender as you enter the premises. A medical practice may use facial recognition to alert the staff about a known hostile patient or for auto check-in, or perhaps to protect sensitive areas such as the maternity ward, allowing access only to known family members.

Most people respond unfavorably when asked how they feel about using facial recognition software that allows other entities to access personal information without consent. However, we have already forfeited a lot of this personal information by agreeing to communicate on the various social media platforms and search engines that collect enormous amounts of data, including images of your face. By now, many of you have uploaded photos to Facebook and noticed how it can automatically tag you in the picture without you making the decision. The same is true with Instagram, Twitter, LinkedIn and others. Other data elements can be associated with these facial images, such as your spending habits, religious affiliations, political views, hobbies, etc. This allows anyone with this software to create customized approaches to how they target you or, worse, treat you differently.

AI in the Exam Room

Today, most healthcare provider organizations have electronic health records (EHR). However, these tools are static databases with algorithms that complement and support humans to complete simple tasks. They do not think for the users; they store data and serve as repositories of information. Now, with the advancement of AI, that factor is changing rapidly. AI today can augment human activity with the ability to sense, understand and learn. AI in healthcare is a collection of technologies that enable machines to understand and learn so they can perform administrative and clinical healthcare functions.

The primary aim of health-related AI applications should be to analyze relationships between prevention and/or treatment techniques and patient outcomes. Privacy policies must catch up to AI to ensure there is no overstepping of boundaries. Thus, the most obvious application of AI in healthcare is data management and its compatibility with the existing EHRs. As with all innovation driven by data, collecting, storing, normalizing and tracing the lineage of the data are the first steps in developing an AI strategy. Today, AI programs are already developed and applied to aid in the diagnosis process, treatment protocol development, drug development, personalized medicine and patient monitoring and care. We are now expecting AI to make its way into eliminating repetitive jobs and to allow for predictive automation.

As AI advances, we will need to consider the creation of ethical standards that are applicable any time patient data are used, with a specific emphasis on patient privacy and accountability for data usage. Now would be a good time to review your patient privacy policies to see how they may need to be updated for changes in your technology, which should also include patient messaging, patient portal, text messaging and others.

The Ethics of AI

Introducing AI into any industry generates several ethical questions:

- What happens when AI shows bias or acts in discriminatory way (see Microsoft's Tay experiment)? An example of this in healthcare could be if the AI started profiling patients with a bad credit score for extra screening before they could schedule an appointment. What if the AI was tracking the race of patients who had balances or missed appointments? AI bias does not have to be intended; it can sometimes evolve based on statistics being collected, especially if the AI is not locked down. For example, let's say 100 patients missed appointments last year. Out of the 100 patients, 30% were born in the month of October. Does this mean that people born in October are awful at keeping commitments, or is this just a random stat with no relevance? The answer would be the latter, but computers don't have critical thinking skills, so it might apply this outcome to future decisions that would treat patients born in October differently.
- How do we counteract inequality and distribute the wealth created by machines? An example of this would be a machine making a clinical diagnosis that would have historically been made by the provider, and the provider would have been paid for his/her expertise to make such a diagnosis. Factors such as the involvement level of the provider and ownership of the AI might be a factor in this example. On the positive side, it could be used to improve capacity, allowing providers to treat patients faster and with better outcomes. As with most innovations that disrupt markets (e.g., Blockbuster vs Netflix), the consumers will respond to whatever creates the greatest value. Capitalizing on it may simply mean embracing it before the competition does. When you consider how disrupters such as Uber and Amazon replaced entire industries overnight, one must always be mindful of change and willing to adapt.
- Can AI have rights? If corporations can be viewed as entities and have rights, can the same be said of machines possessing artificial

intelligence? The legal industry is currently grappling with this question, so this trend is something to watch.

■ How do machines affect our behavior and interactions? Many behavioral health experts have already started to express concerns over the impact that computers, especially social media, are having on our culture and behavior. Evidence is mounting about the link between social media and depression. Some feel it distorts reality and has the potential to make one feel inadequate when comparing their own life to images they see on social media, which are often over-hyped. Isolation from human interaction is another concern. Although there are many unknowns, most experts see too much interaction with computers as being unhealthy. Nevertheless, there is an entire market being created to develop companionship bots (also known as sex bots) for those who prefer having a relationship with a computer over a real human.

■ Who owns the intellectual property developed by AI once its intended use is achieved? As stated previously, AI is either locked or open AI. A locked AI prevents the AI from adapting, whereas open AI is programmed to evolve and adapt. What happens if/when the AI solves a problem that can later be monetized? How about the data used to power the AI? Should the contributors benefit if it was patient data or consumer input? AI innovation will take input data from many sources. Some argue that platforms such as Facebook, Google and Twitter, who aggregate large quantities of data for financial gains, should share these profits with the consumers/contributors. Others argue that no one is forcing consumers to use or share data on these platforms, so these companies are free to do what they want with the data. The compromise may come down to providing advance notice so consumers can opt in or out. Most consumers are willing to accept the trade-off when they know what to expect.

■ In dealing with AI that causes harm, who is at fault? There is currently some movement to mandate that medical AI software and EHRs go through similar FDA approval like most medical devices. The argument for it is to hold vendors accountable for defects that could cause a caregiver to make a mistake. The argument against it is the fact that these are just tools; they don't take the place of judgment. There are also concerns over stifling innovation out of fear of being held accountable for user errors and or an honest defect, which are common when developing new software.

■ What happens to privacy and consent when AI is used for tasks like facial recognition? The current HIPAA laws do not address AI facial recognition, although some argue it falls under the same category as recording or video notice requirements. Signage such as, "This area is under video surveillance for your protection," is how these notices are displayed today. Most ignore them or have become insensitive to them.

■ Some state governments are looking at enacting the "right to be forgotten" legislation. Under this concept, a consumer can demand the deletion of all their personal data. While this initiative seems logical, can corporations honestly ensure they can purge all the data collected on consumers? What about company records that are necessary for audits, etc.? Let's say a patient demands a provider delete his or her records, but the vendor is in control of the data. Moreover, the provider needs these records for his or her protection. While the "right to be forgotten" is a movement to force technology companies to remove personal data that are stored electronically, the issue is not a black-and-white matter. Thus, the industry needs to improve on allowing patients the rights to correct or amend mistakes in their electronic records.

As industries move forward with implementing AI, these concerns (and others) will continue to be new unknowns and opportunities to adapt for the better.

Moving forward with an AI Strategy

As you begin the journey towards AI, it is critical to keep expectations in perspective. Despite current advances, there are significant challenges in this field that include the challenges and options shown in Table 5.1.

From an adoption standpoint, we recommend the following:

■ Learn about and research AI.
■ Create awareness among the stakeholders and providers.
■ Change potentially negative mindsets toward AI with awareness campaigns that have a focus on benefits and value.
■ Educate leadership through attending conferences, workshops, webinars, this publication, etc.
■ Set low expectations at the beginning.
■ Identify easy wins (most critical).

Table 5.1 AI Challenges and Options for Overcoming

Challenges	Options for Overcoming the Challenge
Providers are reluctant to accept AI at the point of care.	Providers will almost always adapt when the benefits and the value for both the patient and caregiver are clear. Focus on the results and benefits. Offer a trial run to demonstrate proof of concept.
Availability of quality data from which to build and maintain AI applications.	At the heart of any AI strategy is the need to have robust data. One option would be to start with the outcome and work back into all the necessary data elements needed to achieve those results. Contrast and compare the current database structure to verify the data are being captured. Most software programs can provide a visual mapping of all the data elements with discrete fields. Vendors rely on subject-matter experts such as providers and nurses to give input on the database structure. For example, what tests typically are ordered for a condition is not something a programmer will know. This must be done as a team consisting of technical and clinical experts.
Missing data streams.	As a follow-up to the above, any gaps in the data elements will need to be addressed. This may mean additional programing or adding the required fields to the intake process.
Limitations of AI methods in health and healthcare software applications.	AI is still in its early stages of development. No one should set unrealistic expectations. Start with something basic leveraging the existing EHR or data repository.

- Embrace cloud computing (see Chapter 2).
- Form an AI workgroup to research and screen vendors.
- Identify gaps in data/capabilities.
- Consider market-based platforms as opposed to self-developed ones.
- Consider enlisting a third-party expert to transfer knowledge and to avoid pitfalls.

Summary

The exponential explosion in the use of AI in healthcare environments compels industry leaders to consider the various applications available for adoption. Although AI delivers many solutions, it is also fraught with multiple problems for patients and providers. Use the ample resources available to educate yourself and your organization on all the potential benefits and pitfalls of the technology. Staying informed and up to date on artificial intelligence will ensure that your organization is using the most current tools available, while adhering to the ethical requirements that this new field imposes.

Chatbot technology today mostly relies on what is called "IF, AND, DO, WHAT LOGIC." If you say THIS, the system will do THAT. An example of this logic might be a patient calling into a nurse line managed by a chatbot. The first interaction with the chatbot would likely include establishing if the person calling is the patient or is calling on behalf of the patient. Next, it might establish if the patient is male or female and if the patient is new or established. If the patient is new, the chatbot interaction will be modified accordingly. Figure 5.3, which shows how patient input and answers are converted to output. The hidden layer is where the programing takes place in accord with the input.

Deep learning uses similar logic as that described above, but there are multiple levels of representation, obtained by composing simple but

Figure 5.3   Chatbot in patient care.

non-linear modules that each transform the representation at one level (starting with the raw input) into a representation at a higher, slightly more abstract level. In simple terms, the outcome gets corelated with the desired result. If the result is not achieved, the AI factors this into the programing so that the machine will continue to improve. A well-known (and real-time) example of this can be seen when we use navigation maps on our phones. These navigations maps know that the desired outcome is the fastest route. Therefore the system is always adapting to current situations based on real-time input based on road conditions being sent back by thousands of other drivers traveling these same roads.

AI Resources

The following are several online resources, some free and some with fees, that are available for getting started:

- Udacity's "Intro to Artificial Intelligence" course and the Artificial Intelligence Nanodegree program at www.coursetalk.com/providers/u dacity/courses/intro-to-artificial-intelligence.
- Stanford University's online lectures: "Artificial Intelligence: Principles and Techniques" at https://online.stanford.edu/courses/cs221-artificial-in telligence-principles-and-techniques.
- ColumbiaX MicroMasters® Program in Artificial Intelligence online course offered through Columbia University at https://cvn.columbia.edu/ content/micromasters-program-artificial-intelligence.
- Microsoft's open-source Cognitive Toolkit (previously known as CNTK) to help developers to master deep-learning algorithms.
- Google's open-source (OS) TensorFlow software library for machine intelligence.
- AI Resources, an open-source code directory from the AI Access Foundation.
- The Association for the Advancement of Artificial Intelligence (AAAI)'s Resources Page.
- MonkeyLearn's Gentle Guide to Machine Learning.
- Stephen Hawking and Elon Musk's Future of Life Institute.
- OpenAI, an open industry and academia-wide deep-learning initiative.

Bibliography

1. Columbus, Louis. 10 Charts That Will Change Your Perspective on Artificial Intelligence's Growth. *Forbes*, January 12, 2019. https://www.forbes.com/sites/l ouiscolumbus/2018/01/12/10-charts-that-will-change-your-perspective-on-artificial-intelligences-growth/#6f8b0a0e4758. Accessed May 2, 2019.
2. Kellerher, Keven. UPS Begins Using Drones to Transport Medical Samples at North Carolina Hospitals. *Fortune.com*, March 26, 2019. http://fortune.com/2 019/03/26/ups-matternet-drones-transport-medical-samples-north-carolina-hos pitals/. Accessed May 2, 2019.
3. Reilly, Michael. Google Now Tracks Your Credit Card Purchases and Connects Them to Its Online Profile of You. *MIT's Technology Review*, May 25, 2017. https://www.technologyreview.com/s/607938/google-now-tracks-your-credit-car d-purchases-and-connects-them-to-its-online-profile-of-you/. Accessed May 2, 2019.

Chapter 6

Improving Patient Engagement with Technology

As the healthcare industry continues to shift toward value-based care, physicians are seeking better ways to deliver timely and effective health and wellness care while improving patient outcomes in the most cost-effective manner. Many physicians have created, or are in the process of creating, patient-centered models of care designed to achieve this goal while creating extraordinarily positive experiences when planning and giving care to their patients and their families. Today, patients have many care options available to them, and physicians need to create patient experiences that stand out from the rest and attract and retain the patients they need. Doing so is a *required competitive differentiator* in today's healthcare marketplace.

Creating extraordinary experiences that result in patients wanting to return for care in the future requires a significant shift in the physician–patient relationship. This higher level of patient engagement with physicians must rest on trust gained through a strong sense of responsibility and accountability to each other and, of course, ongoing communication. This chapter explores ways that healthcare organizations are using information technology to create positive patient experiences that strengthen and sustain patient engagement with physicians.

What Is Patient Engagement?

In its simplest form, patient engagement is when both patients and physicians work diligently together to improve the patient's health. Physicians seek to use their knowledge and experience, along with evidence-based best practices, to develop a plan of care designed to improve a patient's health condition.[1] None of these efforts will matter if the patient does not understand what he or she is being asked to do or, worse, chooses not to participate in his or her care. Therefore, the goal is to engage patients to participate actively in the plan(s) of care so they can recover from their illness sooner and/or attain higher levels of wellness.

In building patient engagement, physicians treat patients with respect by listening to them as unique individuals. Patients then know they are heard and have a say in their healthcare decisions. Likewise, patients listen to their provider's instructions, advice and encouragement and then follow through with making the life changes necessary to improve their health and wellness. Patients who are actively engaged in their healthcare decisions tend to be healthier and have better outcomes.[1] Fundamentally, patients look for physicians who meet the following needs:

- Convenient access with short wait times to receive care (e.g., after-hours and weekends)
- A predictable experience with every care interaction
- Out-of-pocket cost transparency (e.g., deductibles, co-insurance, non-covered services)
- Confidence that their physicians will deliver quality care without harming the patient
- Help with navigating the confusing, questionable and conflicting information available on the Internet
- Ability to manage their healthcare using personal devices in the same way they manage their time, e-mails, finances, etc.

Physicians must align their service delivery approaches with the needs and desires of the people they want to attract. They need to create *extraordinary* experiences that keep these people coming back and telling others about their positive encounters. To help them accomplish these goals, physicians are using information technology to create and maintain positive patient experiences to strengthen patient engagement over the long-term.

Using Information Technology (IT) to Build Long-Term Patient Engagement

Most physicians now have an electronic health record (EHR) system in their organizations. Some are on their second or third generation of EHR as they seek to advance their IT ecosystem. Whatever EHR and other IT systems a physician is using, they must incorporate the following principles to improve patient engagement:

1. Present care plan information, explanations and results on an elementary level so patients can understand what is going on, what actions they must take, how to perform those actions and the expected outcomes of these actions.
2. Set specific, personal and measurable goals with appropriate follow-up to encourage patients to follow their plan of care. Incorporate deadlines and measurable goals and accountability in care plans to encourage active patient participation, like Weight Watchers and similar groups that offer weekly weigh-in checks, and other accountability measures.
3. Make patient care plan information shareable and easily accessible in a single location for the patient and all his or her authorized caregivers across the patient's continuum of care. The EHR is the ideal place for sharing patient care plans, goals, progress and more.

Patient portals are ideal places to share goals, action items, reminders, information and the like with patients. The availability of a single access point for obtaining information enables patients to determine how they want to consume the data and share them with their other physicians, if needed.

Physicians e-connect with patients and families through:

■ Patient portals.
■ Secure messaging.
■ Social media.
■ RFID tracking – patients arrive, mobile greeters give them a tablet, confirm info, point them to the right location, give them a badge, point them to the right location and track who they are, where they are and personalize interactions accordingly.

The following tools are commonly used to improve engagement between patients and physicians:

■ **Patient info portals**. You can provide online profiles with patient information so they can access and review their own health records and data.

- **Online scheduling**. Digital portals with online scheduling services can make it easier for patients to remember to schedule their appointments and book them with ease.
- **Resource libraries**. Provide both in-office and online resources where patients can find more information about wellness initiatives.
- **In-office screens and kiosks**. Connect with patients while they are in your office using interactive signs and digital screens that share health-care advice and wellness tips.
- **Social media**. Encourage your patients to connect with your practice on social media so they can stay up to date with wellness information you share.
- **E-mail and secure messaging**. E-mails with general information are useful for connecting with your patients. Then, use secure messaging to share more confidential information and individualized healthcare notes.
- **Apps**. Both third-party apps and custom apps that you create for your office present opportunities for your patients to track and manage their healthcare initiatives.
- **Wearable devices**. Wearable devices, like Fitbits, are useful for tracking patient well-being in real time and for creating a database related to physical activity.
- **Open-access scheduling.** According to David Levin, M.D., chief medical information officer at Cleveland Clinic, one of the earliest and biggest changes came when the decision was made to make it easier for patients to get in and see their doctors. Now, at all of Cleveland Clinic's family health centers, patients can log on through the patient portal, view their provider's entire schedule and set their own appointments.[2]
- **Patient education**. A key part of ensuring both patient satisfaction and ongoing engagement, Dr. Levin said, is "being sure that patients understand what's going on with them, as well as what's supposed to happen next." To that end, Cleveland Clinic creates appropriate patient educational materials, which can also be accessed online, that run the gamut from follow-up information after individual visits to continuing care information for chronic conditions.
- **Open medical records policy**. According to Lori Posk, M.D., Cleveland Clinic's medical director, Cleveland Clinic has had an open records policy for years, but now everything is getting put online in personal health records. Moreover, since October of 2012 the

organization has been rolling out increasing access to electronic patient information, beginning first with lab results. From January to September of this year, Dr. Posk noted, 3.5 million lab results and images had been made available to patients electronically. Soon, she said, patients will also be able to review their physicians' notes online after a visit, in addition to being able to schedule follow-up appointments.[2]

- **Two-way messaging via patient portal**. The telephone has long been the indispensable tool for communications between doctors and patients, but now communication has been significantly expanded, as well as made considerably more convenient, with e-mail and other electronic formats made available on the clinic's patient portal. Dr. Levin pointed to the ease with which a variety of information can be shared in this manner, noting also that "in a world defined by healthcare reform, we see a big role for this kind of communication in coaching patients and eliminating unnecessary office visits."

- **Patient-reported outcomes**. Taking patient engagement up yet another notch, Dr. Levin said the organization has begun a series of pilot projects in which patients can enter data into their own records. This information, he said, then becomes part of the clinical workflow, enabling doctors to track their patients' progress, and potentially modify their care, between visits.

What Is Gamification?

It might seem like a loaded phrase, but gamification is a simple concept used to engage you daily. Checking your Facebook feed for new updates, using a fitness tracker to log your daily steps and even rating an Uber driver are all forms of gamification. At its core, the practice of gamification involves extracting the elements of gameplay that people find compelling and using them to drive actions and behaviors in non-game settings.

Gamification can be used to attract and retain customers across multiple disciplines, including the pharmaceutical industry. By using core tactics of gamification in their patient engagement programs, pharmaceutical marketers and brand managers can tap into the psychological aspects of game mechanics to create high-value interactions with patients. And when it comes to addressing the issue of non-adherence, gamification for pharmaceutical brands can be a valuable tool to improve patient outcomes and ultimately help the bottom line.

How Can Gamification Be Used to Engage Patients?

Gamification hinges upon hooking users into a digital experience, and, when applied to pharma brands, marketers can effectively keep patients engaged and motivated to take their medications as prescribed. Games work by satisfying several human desires, including reward, status, achievement, self-expression, competition and altruism. The mechanics behind games, from points and levels to challenges and leaderboards, are responsible for addressing these desires. Completing challenging goals, for example, brings a rush of energy and elation that keeps players coming back.

This is where an increased amount of dopamine – the chemical at the center of our brain's pleasure system – comes into play. Dopamine can help drive frequent engagement, which marketers can harness to help educate patients about their condition, their medication and the benefits of remaining adherent.

Six Trends to Take Patient Engagement to the Next Level

As physicians seek to engage more closely and effectively with patients and their families, they will inevitably need to use one or more of the following patient engagement tools:

1. **Data analytics**. The rise of new reimbursement models and the massive amount of clinical data contained in EHRs will create a need for data analytics. This structured approach will be essential in helping physicians manage patient populations and zero in on individual patients at risk. This will help physicians meet their cost and quality targets. Meanwhile, analyses will help form the backbone of targeted patient engagement strategies.
2. **Improved access to patient data**. As mentioned, demand is growing for access to patient data, and various stakeholders have responded. For example, in the private sector, the CommonWell Health Alliance and Epic's Care Quality interoperability platforms enable patients to access their health data, allowing them to self-enroll in the network, link their health records from different care physicians and view their data across the network. On the public side, the federal Office of the National

Coordinator for Health Information Technology (ONC) has been proactive in helping patients gain better online access to their health records. For example, the agency garnered pledges in February from hospital systems and health IT developers to improve consumer access to health records and not block access to data. The latter has been viewed as a problem in the marketplace. All healthcare organizations pledged to share patient records. ONC hopes for a progress check in the next few months.

3. **Longitudinal view of patient care**. Organizations are moving away from the "one doc, one patient, one disease" model to a world of shared decision-making and a longitudinal view of patient care. Health IT and patient engagement will be key to connecting the dots along the continuum of care.

4. **Continued rise of consumerism**. Expect to see more consumerism in healthcare. Physicians are now reorienting toward patients as consumers and emphasizing their connections with community. There are several reasons for this trend. First, physicians are taking to heart consumers' demands for convenience and value because they improve care and outcomes. Those are mission-critical objectives for everyone. Second, they are responding to payers' new reimbursement models linking payments to quality and patient satisfaction. Third, the patient experience has value and can create competitive advantage. Finally, patients, themselves, are seeking value for their healthcare dollar, especially now that millions are purchasing their own insurance and experiencing high – and escalating – out-of-pocket costs. These costs were masked when insurance was more of an employer-paid benefit.

5. **Demand for connectedness**. Consumers are demanding to stay connected with everyone, everywhere, anytime – with technologies customized to their needs and pocketbooks. We must not fall into the trap of thinking that solving the patient engagement problem is all about technology. It is also about meeting consumer expectations of getting and staying connected in an increasingly connected world. Uber is a good, well-known analogy. The company has invested in a lot of technology; however, at the end of the day, the valuable piece is connecting one person with another at just the right time. The same principle holds true in healthcare, for which the useful tools and interesting business models will be about connecting patients and physicians at the right moments.

6. **Impact of demographics and technology diffusion**. The adoption of patient engagement tools will be impacted by demographics and the normal speed of technology diffusion within a market, which generally takes 10 to 15 years. We are still very early in the availability of consumer healthcare technology, including patient engagement tools. That means there is room for the market to grow and mature. At the same time, the oldest members of the "Gen Z" generation are beginning to have children, and this generation demands technology to stay connected and engaged. As a result, demographics will move the needle for patient engagement in the long run. Taken together, demographics and technology diffusion will create a sizeable patient engagement market in the future. Estimating the size of the market may be challenging, however. For one thing, there is no single definition of patient engagement, which often is used synonymously with population health. They are related but different: Patient engagement is an important piece of population health. That is one reason why the patient engagement market may be underestimated. One analysis puts this at $34 billion in 2023 or only around $100 per person in the U.S. Some industry experts think that number is too low, and that the market potential is greater.

Automated communication and accountability tools are becoming vital components of today's EHRs. These tools are designed to improve patient and physician engagement and will continue to change the way patients and physicians interact for improved care.

Summary

Positive and sustained provider and patient engagement can have a dramatic impact, yielding higher physician and patient satisfaction scores, higher clinical quality and higher profitability. As competition intensifies and consumer expectations rise, provider and patient engagement has become one of the most important drivers of success for today's healthcare organization. Information technology will play a key role in improving the success of this engagement for provider organizations. However, whatever technology is deployed, it is NOT the solution in and of itself. Rather, it is one part of the overall solution to improving provider and patient engagement.

Resources

1. Why Is Patient Engagement Important? *Health Term*, July 17, 2019. https://www.carecom.com/why-is-patient-engagement-important/. Accessed February 24, 2020.
2. Rowe J. 5 Ways Cleveland Clinic Improved its Patient Engagement Strategies. *Healthcare IT News*, October 1, 2013. https://www.healthcareitnews.com/news/5-ways-cleveland-clinic-improved-its-patient-engagement-strategies. Accessed February 26, 2020.

Chapter 7

Chapter 7

EHRs and Telemedicine

Ironically, the COVID-19 pandemic began spreading around the world just after we finished writing this chapter. Overnight, the entire landscape of telehealth forever changed, and telemedicine became the top technological focal point for delivering patient care worldwide. Accordingly, we have revised this chapter significantly, as the adoption of telehealth has progressed on a scale never seen before. Telehealth, due to the COVID-19 pandemic, has emerged as the most significant trend since the adoption of EHRs in healthcare by enabling patients to access care when and where they need it. It is dramatically changing the delivery of healthcare and has the potential to be disruptive and transformative. While representatives at hospitals and health systems had been curious about telehealth prior to the COVID-19 crisis, it has now become an essential tool for keeping their doors open and instrumental in responding to the pandemic.

In this chapter, we begin with the basics and move to practical applications for implementing telehealth services. We define telehealth and address its importance, present the business case for virtual care, describe common delivery models, explore regulatory and other compliance matters, provide support in the review of vendor contracts and address pertinent operational issues. We want to help your organization avoid the potholes that may be disruptive as you move forward in the adoption of telehealth programs.

What Is Telehealth?

The Center for Connected Health Policy (CCHP) defines telehealth as follows:

Telehealth is a collection of means or methods for enhancing healthcare, public health, and health education delivery and support using telecommunications technologies.

However, state and federal agencies often differ on how they define telehealth. The Health Resources and Services Administration (HRSA) explains telehealth as:

The use of electronic information and telecommunications technologies to support long-distance clinical healthcare, patient and professional health-related education, public health, and health administration.[1]

Telehealth, at its core, incorporates a wide variety of methods for delivering virtual care. Some systems even use chatbots as opposed to a live provider. (We will discuss chatbots in more detail later in this chapter.) Telehealth should not be considered a specific service. Instead, it is the means to enhance and provide care in a virtual setting from remote locations. The concept and technical capabilities of telehealth are extremely basic and simple; however, there is a longstanding tradition of delivering care at the bedside of the patient. Even before we had hospitals and medical practices, the physician would come to the patient's home and deliver the care in person. The provider–patient relationship is considered very personal and sacred. For many, it can feel awkward if this once longstanding "face-to-face" relationship is now managed over electronic devices. For others (and future generations), this is nothing new. Good or bad, social media has already replaced a lot of our interactions once only possible to do in person. As a kid, if I wanted to get a group of other kids together for a play date, I had to go house to house asking if Johnny could come out to play. Today, kids can organize an event in a matter of seconds and have the announcement reach millions. We can now summon almost any product imaginable from Amazon.com, and it will come for delivery the next day (or the same day in some markets). We no longer go to stores to buy music, movies or process photos. On the business side, virtual meetings using tools like Skype and Zoom have been common for years now. The issue with telehealth has never been about the technology; it has more to do with the personal nature of the provider–patient relationship and whether this can be preserved via a virtual visit. Time will tell, but events like COVID-19 have the power to change the world as we know it, meaning telehealth is now going to be the new norm. So, we will look at it more closely.

Telehealth or Telemedicine?

The term "telemedicine" is most common when referring to traditional clinical diagnosis, monitoring and patient treatment delivered over an electronic device, such as a smartphone or laptop. The term *telehealth* describes a wide range of uses, including non-patient care usages, such as medical education, care team meetings and other related fields of healthcare, including:

- Behavioral health
- Chronic disease monitoring and management
- Dentistry
- Counseling
- Physical and occupational therapy
- Home health
- Disaster response
- Professional education
- Patient education

The population is growing and aging at an accelerated rate. At the same time, many providers are retiring, and fewer students are entering medical school. Thus, we are setting up the perfect storm for major patient access challenges. It is estimated that 10,000 people from the *baby boomer generation* turn 65 years of age every single day, and this trend is expected to continue for the next 25 years.[2] These individuals will consume and demand significant access to medical providers, as almost 80% of all medical conditions tend to show up in the last 20% of a person's life. Some pundits in the industry call this the "silver tsunami" (referring to people with gray hair) which will force the industry to implement more effective ways of deploying healthcare resources while still providing high-quality care to the highest number of patients. The expectations are that telehealth will serve as a key component in meeting these demands.

The Business Case for Telehealth Services

The decision to implement a telehealth program should not be taken lightly. There are many compliance and patient privacy issues to consider.

Typically, most healthcare organizations have general areas of employed expertise, such as clinicians, administrators, case managers and networking staff who can provide valuable input. However, one significant role is often missing: The technical expert who provides the proper insight into the technology infrastructure requirements and advises on the best telehealth solution(s) based on the organization's demands. More concerning is the sheer number of telehealth vendors who rushed into the market to capitalize on the COVID-19 pandemic. Not all platforms are created equal, and many have significant gaps in capabilities, especially with interoperability with the EHR. This inefficiency often leaves both the patient and provider having to work with several systems.

- The telemedicine platform for requesting the visit
- The practice management system/HIE for billing and scheduling
- The EHR system for documenting the notes
- The clearinghouse system for submitting claims
- The third-party lab systems for ordering tests and viewing results

If your team has obvious gaps in the necessary skills to evaluate and/or implement a telemedicine program, it is wise to seek the help and assistance of industry professionals experienced in implementing telehealth programs.

It is also essential to take time in the initial planning phase to assess your organization's clinical, technological and personnel needs. For example, if the clinician is going to work from home, does their home network have the proper security to protect against cybersecurity threats? (See Chapter 3 for tips on how to strengthen home networks.) Do you have devices built for telemedicine equipped with cameras, speakers, headsets, etc.? How about the billing department? Is everyone up to speed on all the billing rules/policies? All these factors are critical to consider when implementing a successful telemedicine program.

Common Telehealth Delivery Models

The American Telehealth Association (ATA) (Business and Finance SIG workgroup) has categorized the various delivery modalities for telehealth services (both traditional and non-traditional) where technology may be used effectively. Table 7.1 is an abbreviated version of the ATA's telehealth delivery model.[3]

Table 7.1 ATA's Telehealth Delivery Model

Name	Description	End Points	Communications Model	Business/Clinical Drivers
Direct Patient Care Teleconsultation (typically clinician to patient sessions)	Video conferencing systems are used to facilitate the remote participation of medical personnel for consultation purposes. Point-to-point or public Internet connections are used. The common format is two-way, interactive, real-time video sessions at a bandwidth sufficient to provide clinical diagnosis.	Healthcare facility to healthcare facility; provider home or office to healthcare facility; healthcare facility or other provider location to patient home; third-party managed care organization headquarters to healthcare facility or patient home.	Real-time video communications. Examples: 1. Psychiatrist at clinic or home providing services to patients at separate, often distant, health facility. 2. GP with infectious disease patient consulting with ID specialist on newest drugs for treatment.	Improved access to care; improved continuity of care; improved recruitment and retention of medical personnel; internal cost reduction (financial savings); increase in retained earnings (reduced travel costs); CO_2 savings (from reduced travel); support of medical home model and ACO payment structure; helps meet quality indicators.
Store and Forward	Services delivered using telecommunications technology but not requiring patient to be present during implementation. Utilizes devices such as digital cameras to capture and transmit still images, for	Healthcare facility to healthcare facility; provider home or office to healthcare facility; healthcare facility or other provider location to patient home; third-party managed care organization	Typically, via dedicated telemedicine computer workstation equipped with software to view transmitted images and related data. Reporting communication is often by e-mail, fax, phone.	Improved access to care; improved continuity of care; improved recruitment and retention of medical personnel; internal cost reduction (financial savings); increase in retained earnings (reduced travel costs);

(Continued)

Table 7.1 (Continued) ATA's Telehealth Delivery Model

Name	Description	End Points	Communications Model	Business/Clinical Drivers
	example of a skin lesion, digitizers or direct digital acquisition of radiographic or pathologic images and transmission of ECG strips.	headquarters to healthcare facility or patient home.	Examples: 1. Tele-dermatologist receives photographs via secure e-mail from GP, interprets and provides treatment recommendations via e-mail response. 2. Tele-radiologist receives radiographic images via secure broadband to PACS workstation, interprets images, renders diagnostic interpretation, dictated report transmitted via secure e-mail to remote clinician.	CO_2 savings (from reduced travel); support of medical home model and ACO payment structure; helps meet quality indicators.
Hospital Care Transitions	Telehealth technology is used to continue to monitor the health of a patient post-discharge for a period sufficient to attain post-discharge health goals and safety objectives.	Care coordination teams at healthcare facilities or management centers to home or transitional care facility (SNF).	Daily or periodic collection of physiological data, subjective health information and any additional information submitted by patients according to protocol reviewed by care coordinator or care management team.	Required quality metrics, public quality reporting requirements, bonus payment structures, patient-centered care delivery requirements, IOM chasms of quality.

(Continued)

Table 7.1 (Continued)   ATA's Telehealth Delivery Model

Name	Description	End Points	Communications Model	Business/Clinical Drivers
Accountable Care Organization (ACO) Model	Primary care becomes coordinator of care and is provided financial incentives to reduce cost of care, improve the health of their patient group, coordinate care of specialists, appropriately use health resources for patients and achieve quality indicators set by payers and primary care together.	Requires an electronic health record for greater depth of implementation, use of telemedicine and e-health strategies to meet goals and objectives, more smart homes and remote monitoring technologies in place. Greater use of telemedicine strategies to coordinate specialists and communication with patients in the home.	EHR and PHR systems (proprietary, HIE and Web-based home telehealth portals).	Improve care efficiency and continuity; facilitate coordination of care, reduction of unnecessary care and return of primary care as the medical home in order to quality for incentive payment.
Home Healthcare Agency Interactive Visits and Remote Monitoring	Assist with achieving PPS low utilization vs. high utilization patient goals for OASIS, used as an efficiency model for home health agencies to do more with less in terms of meeting patient needs. Used for routine checks of vital signs, etc., and to evaluate need to drive out to patient home.	Home connected to the Home Care Agency via phone or Internet for interactive two-way video, remote monitoring and server-based Internet Web portals for sharing of patient data.	Daily or periodic collection of physiological data, subjective health information and any additional information submitted by patients according to protocol – reviewed by care coordinator or care management team.	Reduced costs; fewer hospital visits; increased patient independence, and QOL.

(Continued)

Table 7.1 (Continued)   ATA's Telehealth Delivery Model

Name	Description	End Points	Communications Model	Business/Clinical Drivers
Mobile Health Applications	Applications on smartphones and/or tablets designed to collect health information or provide personal health guidance in many situations and wherever the patient can get connected.	Typically, personal smartphone connected to application server, with information available through authenticated Web portal access or exported to an EHR or PHR.	Cellular, wireless or 3G/4G wireless.	More mobile society, baby boomers reaching critical age points, advancements in smartphone technologies, increase in security procedures, less emphasis on traditional office-based care, increased smartphone adoption and application model. Convenience. Low costs.
Specialist/PCP Co-management of Chronic and Complex Diseases in Rural and Underserved Areas	Videoconferencing systems are used to connect a live, multi-site weekly meeting between specialists and providers.	Group of specialists at university medical center to rural or underserved area or correctional facility primary care providers at multiple endpoints simultaneously for group-based learning. Patients are not seen.	Specialists present on topics of interest, share best practices and hear in-depth, case-based presentations from PCPs. PCPs learn from specialists and their peers and over time become local experts. Supplemented by secure, Web-based communications and information sharing among members.	Reduced professional isolation and improved skills/knowledge base for rural physicians to treat difficult diseases; improved access to specialty care for patients in rural/underserved areas; improved consistency of care.

Regulatory Considerations

Before embarking on a telehealth strategy, it is essential to review and understand the various regulatory considerations. Moreover, because each state regulates telehealth services separately, a review of the multiple requirements affecting the provision of telehealth services is a necessary starting point. Several key issues for consideration include the following:

1. **The provider–patient relationship**. Most states require that a pre-existing relationship exist between the provider and the patient for the provider to dispense telehealth services to the patient. This often means a prior in-person encounter with the patient but in some cases could be a provider's agreement to see or treat a patient.
2. **Patient consent**. Most states require the provider to obtain the patient's informed consent for the receipt of care via telehealth. The requirements may vary from state to state and typically will include a patient *freedom-of-choice* component.
3. **Telehealth provider requirements**. Usually, state licensure boards require the telehealth professional to be licensed in the state where the patient resides (even if the provider lives in a different state). Those expanding their practice to include telehealth should review existing licensure board practice standards, advisory opinions and remote prescribing standards.
4. **Remote prescribing**. This issue continues to evolve and is an area of great variation on a state-by-state basis. Different standards and permissions may exist depending on whether remote prescribing involves controlled or non-controlled substances. Some states require an in-person evaluation before the provider can prescribe drugs on a remote basis. Others, while not requiring an in-person evaluation, may still require a telehealth face-to-face encounter prior to the issuing of a remote prescription. Where states do agree, however, is the prohibition of remote prescribing based on an online questionnaire completed by the patient.
5. **Payer reimbursement and coverage criteria**. Medicare and the various Medicaid programs and commercial payers have requirements that must be met to qualify for coverage. As these requirements are not necessarily consistent, providers are encouraged to review the coverage criteria to ensure that the service that is offered qualifies as telehealth under these payer programs. Further, providers will want to ensure that the correct site of service is coded on the claim.

Fraud and Abuse Considerations

In response to COVID-19, the government temporarily relaxed many of the telehealth regulations to clear the way for rapid deployment and response. However, as we saw during the American Recovery and Reinvestment Act, which offered lucrative incentives for adopting an EHR, the government will always reserve the right to come back and audit later. In fact, to date there have been millions in EHR incentive takebacks and false claims penalties resulting from these audits. Patient privacy is still an expectation without exception.

As is the case in any emerging area of IT adoption that benefits from reimbursement (especially by the federal healthcare programs), enforcement activity is expected to increase. In 2016, the Department of Justice (DOJ) issued a press release of its first False Claims Act (FCA) settlement in the telehealth arena. The settlement entered with Dr. Fry and CPC Associates, a mental health practice, involved the allegation that, although billed as a tele-health service, patients were treated by phone and not via interactive audio or visual communications. Then, in October of 2018, the DOJ indicted seven companies and four individuals for their part in engaging in a telehealth fraud scheme where purportedly $1 billion in healthcare claims were submitted for services that were never rendered. One month later in November 2018, the DOJ issued another indictment related to a physician's prescribing of $20 million in compounded medications to patients who neither requested nor needed them. We can expect scrutiny over billing requirements to increase as coverage for additional types of telehealth is approved.

In addition to the federal requirements, there are state regulations, and each payer may have their own rules. One positive outcome of COVID-19 will be the worldwide adoption of telemedicine on a scale previously unseen, which will likely change the landscape of medicine forever.

In summary, telehealth is not unique when it comes to compliance concerns. Many of the same issues that arise with in-office care can also appear in the telehealth arena, specifically, beneficiary inducements, anti-kickback concerns, fair market value and commercial reasonableness regarding compensation and equipment lease arrangements with physicians (Stark law) and more.

Your Telehealth Program and EHRs

Telehealth technology may be the first interaction (impression) a patient has with a practice/provider/hospital. Therefore, telehealth must be positioned to have a positive impact on the way patients interact and communicate with their providers. If the patient/provider experience is problematic, the consequence could be losing the patient to someone who has a smoother platform. Because of this, organizations will need to have technical expertise with the patient (consumer) as one of the end-users. This is a major shift in how many organizations approach their technical support which today is inward-focused. Many organizations compensate for their lack of technical expertise by asking clinicians to produce workarounds. Unfortunately, patients will expect the platforms to work and work smoothly. Health systems are not set up to provide technical support for patients, yet they will be inviting patients to interact with their networks for virtual care.

In an ideal scenario, the telemedicine platform and the EHR would be fully integrated to give a seamless experience for both the patient and the provider. The EHR is critical to the workflow because it is the legal record, and it will be the primary tool for capturing the charges for the visit. Figure 7.1 shows an illustration of this workflow.

There are numerous case studies of telehealth programs that have failed due to poor technology design and workflow decisions. Moreover, the platform decisions can also make or break the efforts given how interoperability between the various solutions is so critical. In some IT eco systems, there would be as many as 10 to 15 platforms all needing to communicate. Figure 7.2 illustrates the most common systems, which are scheduling, EHR, billing, lab, radiology and communication. (The scheduling, EHR and billing system will be fully integrated into one platform in most cases.)

As noted above, the platform selection process is critical. A failed technology selection can not only set an organization back, it can be very costly.

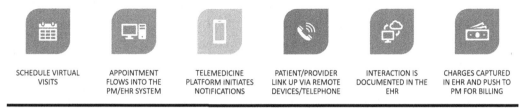

| SCHEDULE VIRTUAL VISITS | APPOINTMENT FLOWS INTO THE PM/EHR SYSTEM | TELEMEDICINE PLATFORM INITIATES NOTIFICATIONS | PATIENT/PROVIDER LINK UP VIA REMOTE DEVICES/TELEPHONE | INTERACTION IS DOCUMENTED IN THE EHR | CHARGES CAPTURED IN EHR AND PUSH TO PM FOR BILLING |

Figure 7.1   Telemedicine platform and EHR workflow.

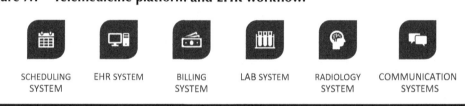

| SCHEDULING SYSTEM | EHR SYSTEM | BILLING SYSTEM | LAB SYSTEM | RADIOLOGY SYSTEM | COMMUNICATION SYSTEMS |

Figure 7.2   Platforms that need to communicate.

Other considerations are the devices. Perhaps the devices are difficult to use, or the data being gathered and transmitted are not good enough to improve the quality of care for the patient. Thoroughly evaluating the telehealth solutions that will be used can help educate clinicians as to what does and does not work well for them.

Privacy and Security Considerations

While patients and healthcare providers are growing more comfortable with sharing medical information online, the risks of being targeted by cyber-criminals are on the rise. The root cause of many telehealth privacy risks centers around the lack of controls on how ePHI is collected, stored and transmitted. Also, negligence on the part of the vendors in terms of the use of technology and disclosure of sensitive personal information can lead to a data breach. An example of this is passive monitoring technology that could be connected in the home or to a person that may unintentionally reveal sensitive or personal information about an individual condition. While this integration is beneficial, it comes with risk, requiring additional efforts to protect ePHI.

Many of the privacy and security challenges are compounded by the lack of clear regulatory guidelines for telehealth, as this is a rapidly developing space with many vendors rushing in to get their share of the market.

While HIPAA policies cover certain aspects, the laws addressing the variety of technologies being leveraged today usually lags behind the laws. Some have suggested that the Food and Drug Administration (FDA) and Federal Trade Commission (FTC) should consider telemedicine as a medical device and require the same level of scrutiny as that of devices that support diagnostic medical care. Patient safety is vital, but this type of enforcement would drive up cost and stifle innovation as many of the smaller vendors could not sustain this level of scrutiny.

Therefore, providers and hospitals should become familiar with some important standards and guidelines before implementing a telehealth program. This should include both state and federal and health plans. Health plans will typically have a document called a "participating provider agreement" that will explain all its expectations and reimbursement guidelines. Medicare also provides similar guidelines. Here is a link to the most recent, which includes the stipulations related to COVID-19: www.cms.gov/new sroom/fact-sheets/medicare-telemedicine-health-care-provider-fact-sheet.[4] Also see Table 7.2.

Table 7.2 Medicare Telemedicine Healthcare Provider Fact Sheet

Type of Services	What Is the Service?	HCPCS/CPT Code	Patient Relationship with Provider
Medicare telehealth visits	A visit with a provider that uses telecommunication systems between a provider and a patient.	Common telehealth services include: • 99201-99215 (office or other outpatient visits) • G0425-G0427 (telehealth consultations, emergency department or initial inpatient) • G0406-G0408 (follow-up inpatient telehealth consultations furnished to beneficiaries in hospitals or SNFs) For a complete list: www.cms.gov/Medicare/Medicare-General-information/Telehealth/Telehealth-Codes	For new* or established patients. *To the extent the 1135 waiver requires an established relationship, HHS will not conduct audits to ensure that such a prior relationship existed for claims submitted during this public health emergency.
Virtual check-in	A brief (5–10 minutes) check-in with your practitioner via telephone or other telecommunications device to decide whether an office visit or other service is needed. A remote evaluation of recorded video and/or images submitted by an established patient.	• HCPCS code G2012 • HCPC5 code G2010	For established patients.
E-visits	A communication between a patient and their provider through an online patient portal.	• 99421 • 99422 • 99423 • G2061 • G2062 • G2063	For established patients.

Source: CMS.gov.

Standards and Guidelines

Many standards, guidelines and best practices have been developed over the years to ensure that the use of telehealth technologies in patient care is managed responsibly. In some regions, telehealth has become the standard of care.

Examples of existing standards include:

■ The Federation of State Medical Boards' Model Policy for the Appropriate Use of Telemedicine Technologies in the Practice of Medicine
■ American Psychological Association Guidelines for the Practice of Telepsychology
■ American Academy of Ambulatory Care Nursing Telehealth Nursing Practice Scope and Standards of Practice
■ American Telemedicine Association Telemedicine Practice Guidelines for:
  – Live, on-demand primary and urgent care
  – Telepathology or tele-ICU operations
  – Core operational guidelines
  – Tele-mental health and video-based online mental health services
  – Store and forward and live-interactive tele-dermatology
  – Videoconferencing-based tele-presenting
  – Diabetic retinopathy
  – Telerehabilitation
  – And more!

Contracting for Telemedicine

New emerging technology presents unknowns and some risk. A good contract is one way to minimize risk and put distance between the vendor and the caregiver if the platform malfunctions. It also protects the buyer from the unexpected. For example, what if the telemedical vendor has a cybersecurity breach that compromises the PHI? You will want the vendor to be responsible for the remediation and any cost liabilities associated with the breach, as you would with any business associate. You can also use the contract to set performance standards, such as response times for support, uptime guarantees if the solution is cloud-based, outage credits for unscheduled downtime and latency issues. An underperforming system/vendor will compromise any telemedical strategy and create risk for the organization. We recommend considering the following terms when contracting for telemedicine services and technology.

- Software warranty must start at go-live.
- Commitment to compliance and regulations, which is especially critical if the vendor bills for telemedicine services.
- Commitment to providing interoperability if the system requires integration.
- Must give a written guarantee to comply with all government mandates.
- Must agree to an acceptance period, which is a set of conditions to meet before the acceptance of the financial obligation.
- Support policy with escalation.
- An uptime guarantee.
- A latency guarantee.
- Outage credits.
- Kick-out provisions to allow for early termination if the performance conditions fall short.
- The vendor must provide version protection, including new releases.
- The vendor must put their source code into escrow if purchasing a license. (This caveat does not apply to subscription services.)
- Consider performance-based payment terms. Here is an example:
  - 10% at signing
  - 10% at the shipment of software
  - 10% at the installation of hardware
  - 10% at the installation of software
  - 10% after testing hardware and software
  - 10% after design-build and validation
  - 10% after successful training and implementation
  - 10% at system go-live
  - 20% at 60 days after system goes live
- The vendor must permit the buyer to re-assign or transfer their license to another owner.
- The vendor must provide the buyer with pricing protection, including caps on support fee escalation.
- The vendor must warrant against defects.
- The vendor must indemnify the practice and defend the practice in the event of a security breach or system malfunction, including cybersecurity incidents.

- The vendor must give the buyer pricing protection for future providers/users.
- The vendor must provide the practice a statement of work (SOW) with a guarantee not to exceed the set amount.
- The vendor must correct any system configuration mistakes at their expense, including missteps in training and implementation.
- The agreement must comply with the Anti-Kickback Statute.
- The agreement must comply with the Beneficiary Inducement Statute and Civil Monetary Penalties law.
- The agreement must comply with the Stark law. Ensure all software and equipment are included in the fair market value (FMV) and commercial reasonableness (CR) review.
- The agreement must comply with state-specific corporate practice of medicine rules.
- The agreement must have a non-solicitation clause.

It is critical to declare the venue and governing law in the state of the buyer. Every contract is different, and terms are always written to protect the seller. While the items listed represent some of the major areas of focus, the list is NOT exclusive, nor should it be taken as legal advice and/or a complete list of terms. Seek advice and feedback from an operational and general awareness viewpoint from a company that deals regularly with technology contracts.

Other Operational Implications

According to a 2018 MGMA survey, patient satisfaction/retention and new revenue sources are the primary return on investment (ROI) incentives for implementing telehealth services.[5] Improved rural coverage, access to specialists and support for value-based care initiatives are additional compelling incentives. Telehealth can also increase provider satisfaction through convenience, flexibility, reduced travel, time management, schedule control and visit slot utilization.

Implementing telehealth capabilities will impact resource needs in a variety of ways depending upon your strategy and delivery model. In some cases, providers and staff will be able to cover broad geographic patient populations more efficiently with less significant travel or redundancy in clinic resources. Other scenarios may require additional clinical or technological staff to support increased volume and patient management and communication. In addition to IT hardware or software, consider other capital investments or savings, such as clinic site rationalization, particularly for rural areas. Additional expenses may be mitigated by savings or financial return in other areas. When developing your strategy and business plan, be sure to include the estimated impact of redesigned care delivery on your existing expenses and infrastructure. Sufficient training and education on new workflows, processes and protocols will be necessary for providers and staff to be successful.

The following is a list of recommendations for communication and education.

1. Start conversations early to gain buy-in from providers and staff.
2. Consider designating a physician champion and other support staff *superusers*.
3. Discuss the value for all stakeholders, particularly patients.
4. Highlight unique benefits for providers, such as the flexibility to work remotely at some point.
5. Provide formal training on technology and protocols to all affected staff.
6. Educate physicians on nuances of conducting an efficient and professional visit.
7. Incentivize providers and others as your compensation model allows.

Most government and commercial payers reimburse for some form of telemedicine services, but many providers and health systems are uncertain of how to implement and manage the necessary changes. As noted, regulations and requirements vary, so it is important to research your payer reimbursement policies as well as any state-specific laws that may govern payer reimbursement policies for telehealth services. Reimbursement rates for most payers are the same as an in-person encounter, which also applies to Medicare. Licensing and credentialing are often more complex with telehealth, particularly when dealing with multiple states or service areas. It is critical to do your research and understand the requirements for your circumstances and strategy.

The Role of Telehealth in the Fight against COVID-19

As stated previously, the COVID-19 pandemic crisis started as we were finalizing the publishing of this book. We felt it was appropriate to add additional information to address how this crisis impacted technology. Hopefully, by the time this book is released, this crisis will be behind us, and this information can serve as a tool for looking back and considering the lessons learned in dealing with COVID-19.

The recent enactment of the Coronavirus Preparedness and Response Supplemental Appropriations Act and the declaration of a national emergency by President Trump provide the tools to allow greater use of telehealth to combat the spread of COVID-19.[6]

The Secretary of Health and Human Services (HHS) issued an 1135 Waiver for "requirements that physicians or other health care professionals hold licenses in the state in which they provide services if they have an equivalent license from another state."[7] The Trump administration also announced on March 17, 2020, that the Act gave the Secretary the power to waive geographic and site restrictions to telehealth in Medicare.[8] As summarized by the Center for Connected Health Policy, the Act did NOT expand the eligible provider list and included an additional qualifier that an eligible provider had to have a pre-existing relationship OR be in the same practice of a physician or practitioner who did have a pre-existing relationship with the patient.[9]

On March 11, 2020, the Secretary received a letter from U.S. Representative Mike Thompson, Committee on Ways and Means, asking for waiver authority granted under the Act to be implemented. The request also specifically states that the "waiver make clear that use of telehealth during the outbreak is not solely restricted to coronavirus patients." Finally, Representative Thompson extended an offer for additional clarification from Congress should that be deemed helpful from the Secretary.

The healthcare industry has increasingly been converting the potential of telehealth into direct care for years. The outbreak of coronavirus, reaching pandemic proportions, and the need for isolation present an unprecedented opportunity for telehealth applications. Expanding the available services for Medicare beneficiaries will help protect the more vulnerable elderly population and allow them to receive routine medical care while remaining in the safety of their homes. Table 7.3 provides the highlights of the March 17, 2020, declaration.

Summary

The global telemedicine market is anticipated to increase rapidly over the next two to three years, according to a *Market Research Future Report*.[11] This report notes that the expectations are that the market will grow at a

Table 7.3 Highlights and Considerations from the March 17, 2020, Press Release

Highlights and Considerations	
Under the 1135 waiver authority, CMS can pay for office, hospital and other visits delivered via telehealth beginning March 6, 2020.	• While many commercial payers are following the lead of CMS in adjusting reimbursement guidelines, it is vital to check the status of payers in your local market. Some of our clients are experiencing variability among commercial carriers.
During the COVID-19 public health emergency period, conventional communication technologies like FaceTime, Skype or Zoom may be used to deliver services without HIPAA penalty.	• We recommend leveraging this option as a last resort. Once the national emergency period ends, an organization will risk HIPAA violations if it continues to deploy these technologies. • Some clients have commented that these services may require contacting patients via practitioners' cell phones. It may be helpful to purchase iPads or other devices and designate a specific contact number to use to prevent sharing practitioners' personal information. • It is essential to document proper consent for each visit. The Medical Association of Georgia has provided a generic informed consent form. • It is also critical to check with your malpractice carrier to verify telehealth services will be covered under your policy.

CMS is separating services into three categories: Medicare telehealth visits, virtual check-ins and e-visits. The CMS toolkit includes a table describing each service, the corresponding	• Medicare telehealth visits can take the place of traditional office visits (CPTs 99201–99205) if audio and visual communications are utilized.
	  • Ensure traditional E&M coding and documentation guidelines are followed.
	  • Can include new or established patients, as the Department of Health and Human Services (HHS) will not conduct audits to ensure an established relationship exists for claims submitted during this public health emergency.
	• Telehealth claims do not require the "CR" modifier, unlike other claims for which Medicare payment is based on a "formal waiver" (i.e., 1135 waiver), as long as the Telehealth Place of Service Code "02" is utilized.

(*Continued*)

Table 7.3 (Continued)   Highlights and Considerations from the March 17, 2020, Press Release

Highlights and Considerations	
codes and patient–provider relationship required. There are several important billing considerations regarding these codes.	• Additional or different modifiers are not required under current emergency waivers, except for the G0 modifier, which is to be used for the diagnosis and treatment of acute stroke.[10] • Virtual check-ins can take place using a wide range of communication methods, unlike Telehealth Visits (i.e., telephone, audio/video, secure text or e-mail, patient portal) and focus on established patients. • Provider time commitment and reimbursement are much lower. • Reimbursement is roughly $15 at the high end (G2012 code, national fee schedule lookup tool). • Note: CMS has not specified place of service and documentation guidelines at this point. • E-visits comprise communication between patients and providers through an online patient portal (CPTs 99421–99423; G2061–G2063).
In addition to carefully selecting service providers and understanding current regulatory guidelines, it is imperative to evaluate operational decisions and impact when deploying telemedicine services.	• Identify which patients and services should be considered for telehealth visits and develop scheduling protocols and workflows for registration, check-in, etc. • Develop adjusted provider and support staff schedules to accommodate telehealth services in coordination with standard services and the impact of COVID-19. • Develop plan for utilizing laptops and remote connections, potentially creating separate workstations in the clinic for telemedicine and standard office visits.

compounded annual growth rate of 16.5% from 2017 to 2023. Factors driving the market include an increase in demand for healthcare services in rural areas and a rise in government initiatives.

Survival of the fittest depends on health systems adopting a telehealth strategy, as otherwise they risk being left behind. Your organization should decide what type of telehealth program to establish to begin this process. You will need to determine how this change will impact the organization. For example, who will be your competitors in offering these services? What will differentiate you from other providers? How will a telehealth program impact your revenue model for clinic(s) or hospital(s)? What are the government-mandated requirements to consider when establishing a telehealth program? These questions and many others should be a part of your telehealth strategic planning process.

In conclusion, transformational forces and events such as COVID-19 will drive an increasing need to invest in these technologies. Moreover, patients will come to expect this technology and will seek out providers who support virtual care. Furthermore, as we continue to push toward value-based medicine and risk contracts, reimbursement pressure will drive the adoption of telehealth. Medicare has already started implementing readmission penalties, and there is growing consumer price sensitivity with a limited supply of physicians. All these factors add up to the perfect storm, which is often the tipping point for much needed change in our approach to delivering care.

Hospitals and medical practices will be turning to telehealth as a tool to increase patient access and as a strategy to lower healthcare costs. If your system lacks a survival plan for providing telehealth services, we highly recommend you consider developing one if you intend to maintain and grow your patient population and increase revenue options for your organization.

Resources

1. About Telehealth. *Center for Connected Health Policy.* https://www.cchpca.org. Accessed May 19, 2020.
2. 2020 Census Will Help Policymakers Prepare for the Incoming Wave of Aging Boomers America Counts Staff, December 10, 2019. https://www.census.gov/library/stories/2019/12/by-2030-all-baby-boomers-will-be-age-65-or-older.html. Accessed May 19, 2020.
3. Telehealth Service Delivery Models, American Telemedicine Association. https://southwestttrc.org/sites/default/files/resources/Telehealth%20Service%20Delivery%20Models(1).pdf. Accessed May 19, 2020.
4. Press Release: Medicare Telemedicine Health Care Provider Fact Sheet, CMS. gov, March 17, 2020. https://www.cms.gov/newsroom/fact-sheets/medicare-telemedicine-health-care-provider-fact-sheet. Accessed May 19, 2020.

5. Telehealth: Adoption and Best Practices - An MGMA Research & Analysis Report. Denver: Medical Group Management Association, 2018. https://www.mgma.com/resources/resources/products/telehealth-adoption-and-best-practices-an-mgma. Accessed May 18, 2020.

6. H.R.6074 - Coronavirus Preparedness and Response. March 05, 2020. https://www.congress.gov/bill/116th-congress/house-bill/6074. Accessed March 17, 2020.

7. Additional Emergency and Disaster-Related Policies and Additional Emergency and Disaster-Related Policies and Procedures That May Be Implemented Only With a §.1135 Waiver. *CMS.gov*, March 15, 2019. https://www.cms.gov/About-CMS/Agency-Information/Emergency/Downloads/MedicareFFS-EmergencyQsAs1135Waiver.pdf. Accessed March 17, 2020.

8. Press Release: "President Trump Expands Telehealth Benefits" https://www.cms.gov/newsroom/press-releases/president-trump-expands-telehealth-benefits-medicare-beneficiaries-during-covid-19-outbreak. Accessed March 17, 2020.

9. Telehealth Coverage Policies in the Time of Covid-19 to. March 16, 2020. https://mtelehealth.com/wp-content/uploads/2020/03/CORONAVIRUS-TELEHEALTH-POLICY-FACT-SHEET-2020-03-16.pdf. Accessed March 17, 2020.

10. Palmetto GBA Jurisdiction J and M Part B Medicare Telehealth Expansion for COVID-19. Webcast: Billing and Coverage. *Palmetto GBA, LLC*, March 24, 2020. https://www.palmettogba.com/event/pgbaevent.nsf/EventDetails.xsp?EventID=BMTNM21786. Accessed May 18, 2020.

11. Vaidya, A. Global Telemedicine Market to Experience 16.5% Annual Growth Rate Through 2023. *Becker's Hospital Review*, September 21, 2017. https://www.beckershospitalreview.com/telehealth/global-telemedicine-market-to-experience-16-5-annual-growth-rate-through-2023.html. Accessed March 31, 2019.

Chapter 8

Advanced Analytics and Dashboard Reporting

> Data is the New Bacon. Data is hot because everything seems to always come back to the data. And there is so much of it – often referred to as Big Data. Data lies at the heart of serving your customers, making decisions, planning, strategizing, and executing or improving on "business as usual."[1]

But how does an organization harness its data?

A healthcare organization must be mature enough to implement rigorous clinical workflows and exhibit astute financial operations to gather the valuable data necessary to produce current, comparative and trustworthy data. By now, many healthcare organizations have adopted information technology at the point of care. They have taken advantage of the incentives handed out by the Centers for Medicare and Medicaid Services (CMS). Through this initiative, a heavy emphasis was placed on the aggregation of data to verify that the organization met the specific objectives required to receive incentives.

While the incentive driver was the adoption of the technology at the point of care, this led to organizations adopting tools that also made data readily available for healthcare leaders to analyze. The maturity stages of adopting this technology involved the keen assessment of workflows, gathering required data elements that seemed to make practicing medicine more cumbersome. However, these demanding processes, if managed and executed correctly, provide healthcare organizations with valuable insight that once was only housed on paper. There was no economical solution to aggregate the information and make strategic decisions on moving an organization forward.

This chapter addresses the various benefits of deploying healthcare dashboards to accomplish advanced analytics to support executive stakeholders in their quest to provide quality healthcare services. Meanwhile, controlling cost and improving patient safety and experiences within their organization run parallel in importance.

Using Workflow Management Tools to Monitor Operations

Healthcare organizations of all sizes are more technically advanced now than they were before the government-boosted uptick in the adoption of technology. This push to adopt electronic medical records (EMR) has strategically merged the aggregation of both clinical and billing data into electronic, reportable data. Higher quality measures have highlighted the need for providers to monitor and improve their clinical performance metrics. Revenue cycle software application developers, working with various models of reimbursements, have also been forced to modify their reporting and claim submission features to meet the requirements of payers. Together, both practice management systems (PMS) and EMRs have accommodated advanced organizations in adopting a new class of enterprise workflow management tools.

However, with all these emerging technologies, many organizations are still operating with inefficient workflows that produce subpar quality metrics and higher costs. The reason is that it is difficult to leverage the many healthcare technology applications that are designed to help their healthcare organization succeed in making sustainable improvements. Clinical and operational data are what today's healthcare leader requires for real-time delivery of aggregate performance data presented in a dashboard.

From a clinical perspective, quality programs under the new Medicare Access and CHIP Reauthorization Act of 2015 (MACRA), which is structured to improve overall patient health and to reward practices that succeed in doing so, requires consistent real-time analysis of an organization's performance in achieving its set goals, for example, an organization's stand-up dashboard specifically for comparing CMS objectives and measures with the organization's progress toward compliance.

Dashboards are also critical for examining revenue cycle management (RCM) performance. Today's PM systems can capture multiple data elements that are not only tied to the financial aspects of the RCM process, but are also tied back to diagnostic and procedure outcomes. In tying into a dashboard that monitors the timeliness of reimbursements, organizations can measure revenue cycle performance and apply evidence-based strategies for improvement. By tracking an organization's performance in key areas, dashboards highlight trends, and even provide alerts that notify the leadership team of diversions from the norm.

The use of dashboards does not stop there. Other functional areas within a healthcare organization can also flourish by observation of their electronic workflows. Scheduling, admissions, human resources, contract management, supply chain and so on have access to vital metrics that can be leveraged to identify areas for improvement that will impact overall performance. When a dashboard is configured to integrate disparate processes and systems into its architecture, the opportunities are unlimited for providing leadership with access to valuable information to enable them to make real-time decisions to manage the course of performance.

In contrast, however, allowing too much data from a healthcare organization to be exposed may cause some leaders and administrators to feel a bit uncomfortable. With transparency being the purpose of the tool, leaders who realize the importance of shared data within their organization are more equipped to change the course of performance more quickly than those who are not employing this asset.

Dashboard Features

To understand the features of a healthcare dashboard requires a look at the problem that the technologies are designed to solve. The primary role of a dashboard is to quickly present data in a meaningful way that empowers end-users to make appropriate decisions. In contrast to analyzing raw data presented in spreadsheets, dashboards replace the "request-and-wait" reporting process. During the reporting request process, managers and clinicians must submit report requests to a clinical/business analyst, then wait for the analyst to compile each report. This process could take a considerable amount of time, in which the circumstances behind the request could have likely changed, thus requiring a new submission.

Analysts rarely had time to analyze the data due to the high demands on them. The end-user then must rely on their own judgment to gauge the data they receive. Whether it is an accounts receivable (A/R) performance report

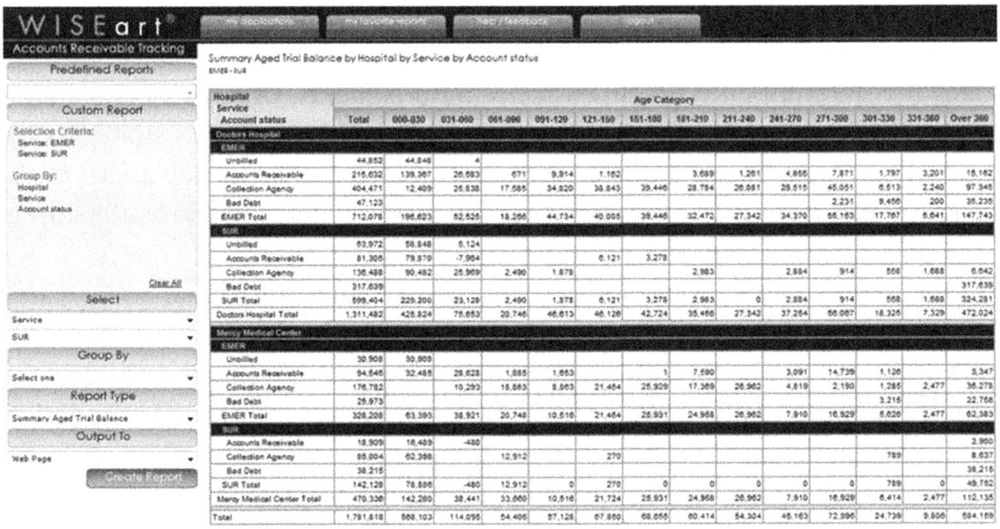

WISEart®

Accounts Receivable Tracking

Summary Aged Trial Balance by Hospital by Service by Account status

Figure 8.1 Sample A/R tracking report. Source: www.wise-ware.com/WISEart.php.

or quality measure statistics, spreadsheets make it challenging to present actionable financial data or evidence-based care. Figure 8.1 is a sample A/R tracking report.

Static reports, using tools such as Access and Excel, occupy an analyst's time with the laborious work of gathering and compiling data. The reports have limited use as an improvement tool because they lack the interactivity and visual presentation of data to help decision-makers make sense of the data presented. Lacking the context for users to understand how to improve, practice evidence-based care and allow providers to compare themselves to their peers or national standards are only a few reasons that static reports fail in the modern setting of healthcare practices.

Five Essential Features of a Dashboard

There are five essential features of a dashboard that ensure that you have the necessary and reliable data.

- **Presents trustworthy data**. If users do not trust the data, they will never use them. This feature is rooted in the processes that define the data and the standard workflows used to define the data, as well as the build/validation process used to present the data.

- **Easy to access**. Having to search an inbox for a report or statistics is a sure way to bury data. Dashboards should be presented as a splash page or in a centralized location on an executive portal.
- **Comparative data**. Trends and benchmarks that are pulled from outside sources to compare an organization's performance instill competitiveness to achieve improved performance. National benchmarks or comparisons to the competition help decision-makers know where they are going in comparison to their peers.
- **Current data**. It is useless for physicians to analyze patient outcomes from outdated reports. Real-time data aggregation is critical in intervening in a patient's care. Timely data allow for users to address obstacles promptly.
- **Clutter-free metrics**. Not all data are relevant data. Overwhelming users with data elements that are unnecessary for decision-making makes the tool more cumbersome and introduces confusion and doubt during the decision-making process.

If dashboards are a representation of multiple sources of data, then it is equally important to invest in a data warehouse to house all the data elements aggregated across multiple disparate systems. Implementing a data warehouse allows data from EMRs, financial systems, human resource applications and device/product inventory systems, just to name a few, to live in a centralized repository for quick and easy access. As above, reliable and timely data are key features of a decision-making tool, such as a dashboard. Having these systems all feeding data into a central warehouse allows dashboards to analyze data; these dashboards are used to display clinical performance and the cost of resources (both human and physical), all while comparing an organization to national standards.

Some key performance indicators (KPIs) and data displayed on enterprise dashboards include, but are not limited to:

- Treatment costs
- Patient wait times (ER and physician practices)
- Patient satisfaction
- Financial performance
- Patient safety
- Length of hospital stays
- Costs by payer
- Readmission rates

- Nurse to patient ratios
- Hospital-acquired infections

Three Critical Types of Healthcare Dashboards

Depending on your organization's goals and strategies, one of the following, if not all, dashboards may have more impact on your strategic decision-making than another. However, we believe all three are very critical for today's healthcare leader.

Physician or Provider Dashboard

Regardless of the level of the clinical provider, there are always valuable data housed in a provider dashboard. Nurse managers need to determine staffing ratios based on patient volumes to provide coverage during the busier times of the practice or hospital wing. Provider dashboards give optics on not only resource demands but also the performance of quality patient outcomes. Whether benchmarked against national standards or the competing organization across town, dashboards can serve to examine employees, communications with and between providers, prescription requests/refills, referrals, patient satisfaction, performance, revenues, costs, etc. Figure 8.2 is an example of a physician or provider dashboard.

Executive Dashboard

Executives who are shaping the strategic direction of a healthcare organization should rely heavily on an executive dashboard. This type of dashboard is ideal for predicting trends, high-level performance and prioritization of change management. It compiles large datasets to display financial metrics, patient admission and departmental performance. This dashboard will rely heavily on well-configured KPIs and relevant data (see Figure 8.3).

Patient Engagement Dashboard

The patient engagement dashboard encompasses all aspects of the patient's experience as they matriculate through a healthcare organization's footprint. The statistics of the patient's continuum of care while under the supervision of your organization (i.e., registration times, referrals, and readmission)

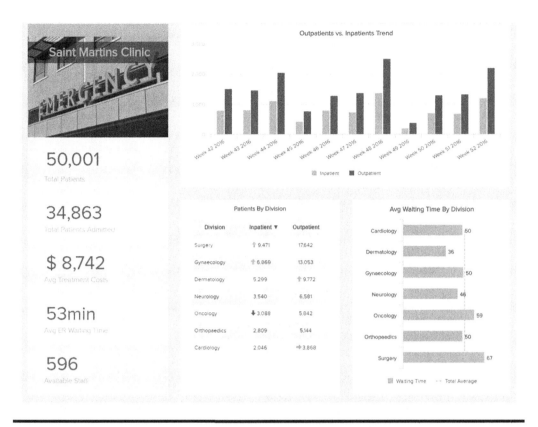

Figure 8.2   Sample physician or provider dashboard. Source: https://www.datapine .com/dashboard-examples-and-templates/healthcare.

should be on display in this dashboard. These data assist organizations in identifying their strengths and weaknesses regarding the patient's experiences, and in evaluating the patient's satisfaction. By combining clinical outcomes and patient satisfaction surveys, these data inputs assist in drawing a picture for organizations to assess their patient experience and how to stay competitive, as patients are more knowledgeable in their treatment and care. Figure 8.4 is a patient satisfaction dashboard report.

Summary

Effective healthcare executives must continually face the challenge of providing the highest quality service while maintaining profitable margins. The effective management and improvement required to identify and optimize the data elements that bring value to the analytics are a precursor to deploying any advanced analytics dashboard. Without the establishment of the

Figure 8.3   Sample executive dashboard. Source: www.datapine.com/dashboard-exa mples-and-templates/healthcare.

proper foundation, too much erroneous data could be in the hands of leaders, which may lead to misjudgments and errors in strategic decisions.

Static reports are unable to adequately meet healthcare executives' performance or predictive analytics needs. Dashboards bridge the gap to provide real-time, organized data, displayed in a meaningful way that allows executives to respond to their organizations' strategic goals.

By displaying layered information, sourced by disparate systems, the presentation of data can span across multiple functional areas to drive high-performing healthcare organizations' operations. If supported by a data warehouse where data elements are tagged to represent critical information, dashboards enable decision-makers to prioritize important events. They can identify areas requiring corrective measures, determine root causes of broken processes, forecast trends and benchmark themselves against other organizations and national standards. The development of these tools requires standard and accurate procedures to ensure the quality of the data that are extracted from processes. While the analytics can assist in the

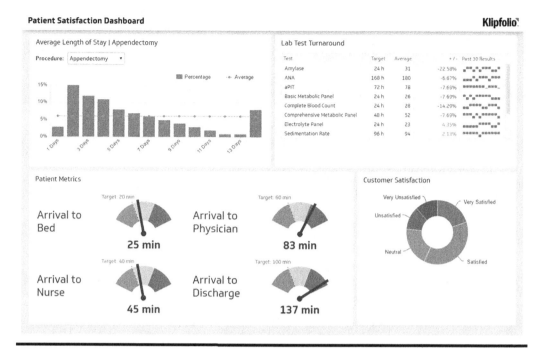

Figure 8.4   Sample patient satisfaction dashboard. Source: www.klipfolio.com/re sources/dashboard-examples/healthcare.

evolution of the optimization of the workflows, there must be adequate effort established well before implementing such a powerful tool.

Data are hot! Like bacon, they're only as good as their source and preparation.

Sources

1. Seiner, R.S. Data is the New Bacon. *The Data Administration Newsletter*, November 15, 2017. https://tdan.com/data-is-the-new-bacon/18796. Accessed February 11, 2020.
2. Lebied, M. How to Improve Your Facility Management with Healthcare Reports. *Datapine Blog*, May 11, 2018. https://www.datapine.com/blog/healt hcare-report-benefits-and-examples/. Accessed February 13, 2020.
3 Leconte, P. 4 Types of Healthcare Reporting Dashboards to Copy. *ClearPoint Strategy*. https://www.clearpointstrategy.com/healthcare-dashboard/. Accessed February 13, 2020.

4. Ghazisaeidi, M., Safdari, R., Torabi, M., Mirzaee, M., Farzi, J., Goodini, A. Development of Performance Dashboards in Healthcare Sector: Key Practical Issues. *Acta Informatica Medica*, Published online October 5, 2015. doi:10.5455/aim.2015.23.317-321. https://www.ncbi.nlm.nih.gov/pmc/articles/PMC4639357/. Accessed February 13, 2020.
5. Interactive Healthcare Dashboards Are Gaining Momentum. *Healthcare Catalyst*, March 10, 2015. https://www.healthcatalyst.com/value-of-healthcare-dashboards. Accessed February 13, 2020.
6. Curtiss, S. The Unsung Benefits of HIT Dashboards. *Healthcare IT News*, October 07, 2011. https://www.healthcareitnews.com/blog/unsung-benefits-hit-dashboards. Accessed February 13, 2020.

Chapter 9

Interoperability

According to the Healthcare Information and Management Systems Society (HIMSS), "interoperability" is defined as the ability of different information systems, devices and applications (systems) to access, exchange, integrate and cooperatively use data in a coordinated manner, within and across organizational, regional and national boundaries, to provide timely and seamless portability of information and optimize the health of individuals and populations globally.[1]

Healthcare IT is continuously evolving, and with that comes an increasing amount of disparate systems and data points that healthcare organizations must utilize in order to provide the best patient care. Most, if not all, healthcare organizations have many different EHR platforms that are not able to provide tangible data from one system to another because they are not interconnected. The exchange of information in healthcare IT systems is paramount towards the advancement of quality of care and efficiency. Recent federal regulations have now mandated the promotion of interoperability to demonstrate Meaningful Use in order to qualify for federal incentive payments. The Centers for Medicare and Medicaid Services (CMS) now require providers to use 2015 edition certified EHR technology (CEHRT) in 2019 to demonstrate Meaningful Use to qualify for federal incentive payments. According to CMS, "This updated technology includes the use of application programming interfaces (APIs), which have the potential to improve the flow of information between providers and patients." CMS also stated, "Patients could collect their health information from multiple providers and potentially incorporate all of their health information into a single portal, application, program, or other software." Changing the Meaningful Use program will increase flexibility and reduce burden, and it will also "emphasize measures that require the exchange of health information between providers and patients," CMS explained. Furthermore, providers will be incentivized to ensure that patients can easily obtain their own medical records electronically.

Levels of Interoperability

There are many barriers to interoperability, and often these barriers are due to the lack of standardization of implementation and integration amongst the multitude of systems available in the healthcare IT market. Interoperability, according to HIMSS, enables healthcare IT systems to exceed organizational restrictions and promote effective healthcare delivery to patients. HIMSS defines four levels of interoperability.[2]

Four Levels of Interoperability

Foundational (Level 1) – establishes the inter-connectivity requirements needed for one system or application to securely communicate data to and receive data from another.

Structural (Level 2) – defines the format, syntax and organization of data exchange including at the data field level for interpretation.

Semantic (Level 3) – provides for common underlying models and codification of the data including the use of data elements with standardized definitions from publicly available value sets and coding vocabularies, providing shared understanding and meaning to the user.

"New" Organizational (Level 4) – includes governance, policy, social, legal and organizational considerations to facilitate the secure, seamless and timely communication and use of data both within and between organizations, entities and individuals. These components enable shared consent, trust and integrated end-user processes and workflows.

For interoperability to work, systems sources must be able to process the data and provide the analytics to organizations, clinicians and the patients in the end. Making sure that patient data is easily accessible, reliable and HIPAA compliant is *critical* for healthcare networks to meet CMS initiatives and value-based care requirements. A well-informed patient is a better patient.

On March 06, 2018, CMS Administrator Seema Verma announced a new initiative from the Trump administration, "MyHealthEData." According to a 2018 EHR intelligence article,

> the initiative is intended to give patients more control of their own EHR data and will do this by breaking down existing barriers to health data access and use. Patients will have access to their own EHRs through the device or application of their choice, stated CMS.[3]

CMS also plans to improve patient access to health data through the following efforts:

- CMS is requiring providers to update their systems to ensure data sharing.
- CMS intends to require that a patient's data follow them after they are discharged from the hospital.
- CMS is working to streamline documentation and billing requirements for providers to allow doctors to spend more time with their patients.
- CMS is working to reduce the incidence of unnecessary and duplicative testing that occurs as a result of providers not sharing data.

A recent 2019 report titled "Sharing Data, Saving Lives: The Hospital Agenda for Interoperability" from the American Hospital Association (AHA) demonstrates that healthcare organizations now realize it is time now to provide the most complete, up-to-date, real-time healthcare data to their patients.[4] This access will help deliver better coordinated patient care and safety. Healthcare IT is continuously evolving to help meet these new standards, but organizations can also help do their part, and get involved with the HIMSS HIE community for roundtable discussions. The "Call to Action" was championed by HIMSS's Interoperability and HIE Committee. Their work initiated the creation of the Interoperability Initiatives Environmental Scan. This committee, according to HIMSS,

> focuses on the advancement of standards-based interoperability and emerging health information technologies that lead to impactful health information exchange. As the healthcare landscape evolves, interoperability is a key driver towards achieving secure and accessible information, as well as realizing lower cost and higher quality care.[5]

Summary

While interoperability will continue to be in the limelight in 2020 and beyond, many obstacles still exist, such as non-standardized patient data, changing quality incentives and secure efficient electronic data exchange among the various systems. It is critical for healthcare organizations to continue to focus on increasing interoperability. They must help facilitate effective ways to clear the path to increased interoperability and high quality of care for all patients. Providers must get involved and become proponents of interoperability.

Sources

1. HIMSS. *HIMSS Dictionary of Health Information Technology Terms, Acronyms, and Organizations.* Boca Raton, FL: CRC Press. 2017.
2. HIMSS. What is Interoperability? https://www.himss.org/what-interoperability. Accessed January 22, 2020.
3. Monica, Kate. MyHealthEData Initiative to Improve EHR Patient Data Access. *EHR Intelligence*, March 6, 2018. https://ehrintelligence.com/news/myhealt hedata-initiative-to-improve-ehr-patient-data-access. Accessed January 22, 2020.
4. AHA. Sharing Data, Saving Lives: The Hospital Agenda for Interoperability, January 18, 2019. https://www.aha.org/system/files/2019-01/Report01_18_19 -Sharing-Data-Saving-Lives_FINAL.pdf. Accessed January 22, 2020.
5. HIMSS. HIMSS Call to Action: Achieve Nationwide, Ubiquitous, Secure Electronic Exchange of Health Information, October 11, 2017. https://www.him ss.org/resources/himss-call-action-achieve-nationwide-ubiquitous-secure-ele ctronic-exchange-health. Accessed January 22, 2020.

Chapter 10

Vendor Contracting and Negotiations

From time to time, practices and hospitals face the task of acquiring and implementing a new electronic health record (EHR) system. Some may find that their current system does not align with their scalability, requirements or the vendor support needed by the organization. When system replacement is inevitable, organizations need to recognize that a new system is not a cure-all for the issues of the past. Replacing an EHR is often more complicated than the implementation of the original one; thus, your organization must invest in the planning needed to define business and user requirements, implementation and integration strategies.

Whether you are reviewing a new information technology (IT) vendor contract or negotiating new terms and conditions of an existing agreement, there are many key factors to consider. Every year practices and hospitals commit financially to vendor contracts without fully understanding the terms and conditions of their obligations. The good news for purchasers of EHR systems is that the marketplace is extremely competitive and, as a result, it is a buyer's market for those willing to put forth the effort and take the time to do their due diligence. However, negotiating with vendors involves much more than just asking for a reduction in price.

Negotiating your new contract should consider all aspects of the client–vendor relationship and the practice's future requirements. Too often, organizations move from one vendor contract to another without proper planning, and most contracts favor the vendor. Therefore, many of the terms and conditions must be renegotiated by the client to neutralize or amend them to benefit the client.

Vendors strive for success as much as you do; however, they will not volunteer to offer more favorable terms and conditions to their client. Most vendors will consider compromises and will work with you to address your concerns regarding the contract, but the buyer must know what to ask for and how to go about negotiating the terms.

If you decide to accept the standard contract terms without negotiation, you assume all the risk with little recourse. Trying to resolve a contract dispute at the time of a breach is less efficient than negotiating an agreement with appropriate safeguards before signing on the dotted line.

The Fundamentals of Negotiating Vendor Contracts

It is difficult to negotiate contracts if the balance of power leans toward the vendor. Since vendor contracts are usually one-sided, the organization needs to protect its interests. In order to have a positive outcome when negotiating your vendor contract, you must first understand the fundamentals of negotiation. Here are ten fundamental rules to help you successfully negotiate with your vendor.

1. The most fundamental rule in the art of negotiation is learning to listen. Listen to the vendor and understand what they want to carry out and communicate what you want to accomplish.
2. Be prepared and do your research before negotiations. Ask questions and get as much information as possible throughout the negotiation process. Understand the needs of your organization and those of the vendor.
3. Do not accept the standard *boilerplate* contract until you weigh the risks and potential costs. It is important to remember that, to at least some degree, every agreement is negotiable. You may not get everything you want, but it is essential to understand your end goal, which is to secure concessions that offer you the greatest amount of protection from liability.
4. Always ensure that the proper parties are identified. Be certain that you are working with a person who has the authority to negotiate contracts.
5. Avoid bad-faith negotiations. Do not commit to the contract in exchange for a special requirement you do not expect to get. The vendor may call your bluff and agree to the conditions.

6. Don't negotiate against yourself. Always wait for a counteroffer.
7. Be reasonable. Negotiating is about compromise and achieving a balanced agreement for both sides. Both parties should view each other as partners who seek to reach a mutually agreeable outcome.
8. Create a list of all issues that matter most to your organization. When reviewing your priorities, be sure to ask yourself: "Is this a *must-have* for our organization, or is it a *nice-to-have* element?" Know your bottom line, so you know when to walk away.
9. Never tell a vendor they are the vendor of choice (VOC). The vendor should feel like they are trying to win your business. Establishing this leverage will help you with your negotiation strategy.
10. Negotiations of your contracts are not singular events. Most negotiations occur repeatedly.

Understanding Types of Vendor Contracts

The first matter to understand about vendor vetting and cost comparison is how software gets licensed to a buyer. One major misconception of software is to do with ownership and rights to use. In most cases, the buyer NEVER owns the software; they just hold the right to use it over a period. This area can be extremely confusing, but it is critical to understand as it will have a profound impact on the cost of ownership and the right to use the software. Table 10.1 is a list of types of licenses and their descriptions.

Sample Vendor Contract Language

It should come as no surprise to hear that vendor contracts do not have the client's best interests in mind. This is not to say the vendor is trying to beat the purchaser out of a good deal; it means that vendors have a lot at risk also, and they can be easy targets for lawsuits. Thus, it is good to have a vendor partner that has protection from clients that bring unwarranted lawsuits against them, putting them and the clients they support in jeopardy. It is never, under any circumstances, in a vendor's best interest to have a dissatisfied client. Most vendors that are serious about staying in business will exhaust all reasonable efforts to keep their clients happy. Future sales depend on it.

Table 10.1 Types of Vendor Contract Licenses

License Type	Description
Term license	Under this arrangement, the vendor sells you the license, but at the end of the term, you MUST repurchase the license. The right to use the software is only for a specific time.
Provider/user license	A provider/user licenses are generally a one-time fee, but the vendor will charge an annual maintenance fee to keep the licenses current. This is the MOST traditional method used today; however, the market has been shifting to subscription arrangements. The annual maintenance fee will generally average 15–21% of the software purchase price.
Leased license	A lease is a form of financing but can create significant risk. Under this option, the leasing company will generally pay the vendor 100% of the total value, including future costs upfront. If the vendor discontinues their product or underperforms, the practice is still financially obligated to the leasing company. Never allow a leasing company to prepay for vendor services not rendered and without prior approval.
Application service provider (ASP)	The APS is often confused with hosting/subscription, but this option is essentially the same as a traditional user/term license; however, the vendor manages the system for you in their datacenter. Over time, this is usually the most expensive option.
Hosting	Hosting and ASP are almost identical, but under this option, the software and infrastructure can get bundled. Some vendors host directly, while others subcontract this service to datacenter partners.
Subscription	Subscriptions have become one of the more popular options because there is usually no up-front cost and all the monthly maintenance, future updates and hosting are in the monthly subscription fee. While this choice is often the most economical, it requires giving up the most control.

It is also important to be very respectful and professional during the negotiations, never pushing a vendor to the point of being unreasonable. A vendor will be relied on for several years. Therefore, mutually acceptable terms and conditions should be the end goal. With sufficient information and understanding, a win-win contract is achievable.

Table 10.2 provides some critical contract requirements and sample language to consider. Note: This list of terms is not all-inclusive. The sample contract language should NOT be regarded as legal advice, nor should this take the place of using an outside attorney or expert in vendor contracting.

Table 10.2   Contract Requirements and Sample Language

Contract Requirements	Definition and Sample Contract Language
Acceptance period	An acceptance period is one of the most important requirements for contracting. The acceptance period states that you will agree to enter a contract but will not be accepting the contract until certain conditions are satisfied and confirmed. **Sample Contract Language:** *Client will accept the Software and System ninety (90) days after the successful installation, implementation and use of each module pertaining to the Software and System. Software not properly installed, or software installation not completed by the Vendor (including System third-party software), will be rectified at the Vendor's expense, including travel expenses for on-site work.* *The parties will agree upon an "Acceptance Plan" as part of the Software Installation of the Software and any "Programs." The Acceptance Plan will include implementation team training for Client personnel and the verification and confirmation of performance in accordance with the documentation and specifications of the Software. The Vendor represents and warrants that the media and other information provided by Vendor for the Software Installation will include, among other items and information, sample data designed to assist in testing and verification that the System is successfully installed and performing specified procedures meeting all published specifications for the current version of the Programs.* *The Acceptance Plan will include at a minimum of five (5) levels of review, as stated below:* 1. *Level 1 Software reviews to ensure that the information, screen and data flows represent those shown in the Documentation.* 2. *Level 2 Software reviews to determine that data elements within the applications are consistent with the Documentation.* 3. *Level 3 Software reviews to determine that all edits, calculations and logic are consistent with the Documentation.* 4. *Level 4 Review to determine that all reports, both online and batch, daily and periodic, are consistent with the Documentation. Also, all data transfer or interfaces within the scope of this Agreement, the Addendum and all Appendices are functioning per specification.* 5. *Level 5 Review to determine that the performance of primary documented operations procedures produces the results described in the documentation.*

(Continued)

Table 10.2 (Continued)   Contract Requirements and Sample Language

Contract Requirements	Definition and Sample Contract Language
System implementation	A successful implementation will make or break the project. You should expect only the most qualified staff working on your project. **Sample Contract Language:** *All personnel serving on the implementation team/trainers must have a minimum of two (2) years of employment with the company in their current role. The Client does not agree to accept and will not be obligated to accept any trainers or other personnel providing service hereunder with less than two (2) years of implementation experience. The Client may request, and Vendor will provide from time to time substitute staff if required by Client.*
Assignments under a merger, acquisition, buy-out, name change, corporate reorganization, a successor organization, a parent or subsidiary, and another entity within the organization	Software is non-transferable! This restriction is a problem for most medical practices in that, one day, the practice may be sold or acquired by another owner. It is imperative to make sure your vendor allows you to transfer your software contract under any circumstance. **Sample Contract Language:** *Notwithstanding any other term or condition in the Agreement, Vendor will allow and hereby consents to the assignment of the Software and System under any of the following conditions or any of the following organizations: merger – to the successor, acquisition – the buyer, buy-out, name change, corporate reorganization, successor organization, subsidiary or affiliate, to another entity within the same organization as Client.*
Data conversion file	The retrieval of your data conversion file should be spelled out in your contract to avoid any surprises when requesting your data to move to another vendor. The terms should include file format and a cap on the amount the vendor can charge. Many vendors charge thousands of dollars, some upwards of $20,000, so make sure to discuss and document these details before signing on the dotted line. **Sample Contract Language:** *Upon the expiration or termination of the Agreement, and provided Client is not in default under the terms of the Agreement, Vendor will provide a complete and secure (i.e., encrypted and appropriately authenticated) downloadable file of the data in an industry-standard programming language, including all schema and transformation definitions and/or delimited text files with documented, detailed schema definitions along with attachments in their native format at a rate NOT to exceed $1,500. The data conversion file will include all patient demographics, health information, imaging, financial data and medical record documentation.*

(Continued)

Table 10.2 (Continued) Contract Requirements and Sample Language

Contract Requirements	Definition and Sample Contract Language
Future upgrades, new releases, version changes, mandated modifications	Never buy any system without an agreement obligating the vendor to provide future system upgrades. Unexpected mandates can happen without notice. The vendor must conform to these requirements and make sure their system stays modern and current. Vendors have been known to sell a version of software, and then later discontinue it, requiring their clients to purchase the upgrade. This scheme should not be allowed, because it is almost certain that vendors will have to provide future upgrades to stay in compliance with government mandates. ***Sample Contract Language:*** *The Vendor will provide to Client continuous and unlimited use and right under this Agreement and Addendum to upgrades, new releases, version changes, mandated modifications and patches to the Software and System under the Service Agreement, the Agreement and this Addendum at no additional cost. Training and installation to support the new releases/upgrades/patches will be covered under the standard maintenance agreement. The Vendor will provide continued support for previous versions of its software for a period of ten (10) years. Additionally, the Client will not be charged for any mandatory software modifications to meet any and all compliance requirements (federal, state or local).*
Third-party software	Most vendors rely on third-party software to run their applications. For example, most vendors will recommend a specific operating system or a database, such as Microsoft Squeal or Oracle. The vendor must be responsible for how their software performs on these third-party components and must provide the necessary troubleshooting to solve issues. ***Sample Contract Language:*** *The Client expects the third-party software recommended by the Vendor to perform as required and to be compatible with the application. The Client will use commercially reasonable efforts to purchase the recommended third-party software in accordance with the Vendor's requirements. The Vendor will pay the replacement cost or cost to purchase alternative third-party software if the recommended third-party software does not meet the requirements or if it compromises the performance of the Software or System.*

(Continued)

Table 10.2 (Continued)   Contract Requirements and Sample Language

Contract Requirements	Definition and Sample Contract Language
Cybersecurity breach	Vendors should be held responsible for any breaches caused due to defects in their software and/or staff working on behalf of the client. ***Sample Contract Language:*** *Vendor will be responsible for any security breaches caused by defects in their software and/or staff working on behalf of the Client. In the event of a security breach, vendor is obligated to cover any damages or fines associated with the breach notification as well as any penalties incurred by the practice as a result of the breach. Vendor will also promptly notify the practice of any breach and will become party to the business associate agreement (BAA).*
Data mining	Vendors should be restricted from mining or accessing your data without prior approval. ***Sample Contract Language:*** *Client does not allow any access to its clinical content and does not authorize the Vendor to conduct any data mining without authorization.*
Audits	Occasionally, a vendor may conduct an audit to ensure their system is being used in accordance with their policies. The vendor should be required to provide prior notice and state the reason for the audit. ***Sample Contract Language:*** *Vendor must notify the Client thirty (30) days prior to an audit by Vendor and state the reason for the audit. All confidentiality provisions will apply to any such audit.*
Access	Except for routine support, vendors should provide advance notice before accessing your system. ***Sample Contract Language:*** *The Vendor must seek prior approval from Client before accessing the Client's server or workstations.*
Government mandates	Vendors are expected to meet federal compliance standards on a myriad of levels. It is not possible to define these standards herein because they are always evolving. A vendor that is committed to staying in the market will commit to meeting and conforming to these standards. ***Sample Contract Language:*** *The Vendor will comply with all government mandates and standards and will modify the Software accordingly at no additional cost to Client.*

(Continued)

Table 10.2 (Continued)   Contract Requirements and Sample Language

Contract Requirements	Definition and Sample Contract Language
Corporate compliance	Compliance varies by vendor, but you should always include any corporate compliance policies necessary for suppliers to follow. **Sample Contract Language:** *Client has developed and implemented a Corporate Compliance Plan to ensure all business activity is conducted in accordance with all federal, state and other laws and regulations as appropriate. Vendor hereby agrees that it will comply with Client's Compliance Plan and will conduct its business in accordance with all federal, state and other laws and regulations as appropriate. The parties warrant that they are in good standing with all federal and state programs and that they are qualified, licensed, registered and/or certified in conformity with federal and state laws and regulations. Should either party's status change, that party will notify the other party immediately, and the party that is notified will have the right to terminate this Agreement immediately. The parties agree to not knowingly participate in any activity under this Agreement or in any aspect of our relationship that may constitute or be construed to constitute a violation of federal or state law regulation, including but not limited to improper arrangements or referrals under the Ethics in Patient Referral Act, Title 42 of the United States Code Section 1395nn (a.k.a. the Stark law), the federal anti-kickback statute, Title 42 of the United States Code Section 1320a-7b(b), or the Health Insurance Portability and Accountability Act of 1996, 104 P.L. 191, 110 Stat. 1936 (1996). We agree to take all reasonable precautions to avoid the same.*
Payment terms	Vendors will generally require their clients to pay 50% upon contract signing and 50% 30 days after they ship the software. This term is unacceptable. The vendor should base their payment terms on actual deliverables and accomplishment. Using a timeline based on dates does not ensure the system is working before payment is expected. Payments should be based on project milestones. Here is an easy example of a reasonable payment term policy. **Sample Contract Language:** *Payment Terms and Conditions:* • *20% down at contracting* • *20% at delivery and install* • *20% after training* • *20% at go-live* • *20% thirty days after successful go-live* • *Subscription/Service/Support fees start at go-live*

(Continued)

Table 10.2 (Continued)   Contract Requirements and Sample Language

Contract Requirements	Definition and Sample Contract Language
Governing law	Every vendor contract states governing law to be in the state of the vendor. Should an issue arise requiring legal action, you would be required to travel to the state of the vendor to take action. Most vendors will agree to move governing law to the state of their client. A reasonable compromise would be to select a state other than where the vendor or practice is located to make it mutually inconvenient to go to court. We strongly recommend moving governing law to the state where the software will be used. **Sample Contract Language:** *This Agreement will be deemed to have been made in the state of (YOUR STATE) and will be governed by and construed in accordance with (YOUR STATE) law. The parties agree to submit all disputes arising out of this Agreement, including its interpretation, exclusively to the state or federal courts of (YOUR STATE).*
Future providers	Now is the time to get an understanding of how the vendor will charge you for future providers. Once you sign the contract, you will no longer have any leverage to secure discounts. This would be an excellent time to have your vendor agree to future pricing. **Sample Contract Language:** *Vendor acknowledges that Client will experience economies of scale of adding future users/providers and agrees to allow Client to have future provider/users at the same percentage of discount based on current day published pricing Increases to support fees. The Vendor can only increase its support fees at the rate of one percent (1%) less than CPI. Additionally, the Vendor cannot look back at more than a one (1) year period if the fee is not increased.*
Support fees	Many vendors will start charging monthly support fees once the contract is signed. You should never begin to pay for support until the system is successfully installed to your satisfaction, and you can verify that requirements from the acceptance period have been fulfilled. **Sample Contract Language:** *Support will be charged applicable to what is installed. Client's obligation to make support fee payments will commence ninety (90) days after the successful installation, implementation and use of the software and system. If the practice is installing multiple modules, Vendor will only charge Client support for the portion installed commencing ninety (90) days after the successful installation, implementation and use of each such module pertaining to the Software and System.*

(Continued)

Table 10.2 (Continued)   Contract Requirements and Sample Language

Contract Requirements	Definition and Sample Contract Language
Interfaces	All vendors offer and provide interfacing. The interface is always a two-party dance between two vendors. Conflicts are frequent, and the vendor can even try to sabotage the other as a way of discouraging interfacing with competing products. Most interfaces can be verified before contracting; however, your contract must hold the vendor accountable and responsible for ensuring the interface stays in working order after the sale. ***Sample Contract Language:*** *Notwithstanding any provision of Section 7 or elsewhere in the Agreement, the Vendor represents and warrants to Client that Vendor will for each Interface purchased by Client perform, support and troubleshoot the Interfaces as a part of the annual maintenance agreement. Vendor will support modifications and version changes to Interfaces at no additional cost to Client. Vendor will provide any Interface already written at no additional cost to Client. Vendor will refund the cost of the Interface if it becomes non-functional and is not corrected within ninety (90) days by Vendor after notice by Client.*
Disabling software	Some vendors will install disabling software that will allow them to shut off your system remotely in the event of a dispute. A vendor should never be allowed to shut off your system under any circumstances. They can refuse to provide support, but shutting off the system should be strictly prohibited. ***Sample Contract Language:*** *Under NO circumstances can Vendor disable or shut off Client's system.*
Warranties	The warranty provided by the vendor is critical to understand and to review thoroughly. Most vendor warranties only last for 90 days, and almost all of them will start at the signing of the contract. In some cases, the warranty expires before the installation of the software. A warranty should only begin after the software goes live and has met the requirements of the acceptance period. ***Sample Contract Language:*** *Vendor guarantees, represents and warrants to Client that Vendor will correct or repair any error, malfunctions or performance defects or provide a reasonable substitution to the Software within ninety (90) days ("Error Correction Period") after Vendor reports such error, malfunctions or performance defects to Client ("Error Notification Date"). If Vendor is not able to correct or repair such error, malfunctions or performance defects in the Software within the Error Correction Period or cannot correct or install a reasonable substitution within the Error Correction Period, Vendor will pay and refund to Client all expenses paid to the Vendor, including Hardware and expenses paid for professional services, including travel expenses.*

(Continued)

Table 10.2 (Continued)   Contract Requirements and Sample Language

Contract Requirements	Definition and Sample Contract Language
Stimulus incentives (MIPS/MACRA)	Client should only choose an EHR vendor that is certified. EHR vendors certified to the standards set forth by the ONC can support you in all four performance categories for MIPS. **Sample Contract Language:** *As part of its standard support, Vendor will provide the following to the Client so long as the Client is receiving Software Maintenance under the Agreement:* a. *All versions of the Software necessary to satisfy all requirements in order to be a Certified EHR for use by the Client and qualify to receive all of the Medicare incentives available under HITECH Act, including MIPS and MACRA.* b. *All implementation, training, data conversion and other services that may be necessary or appropriate to reasonably assist the Client in implementing each of the Certified EHR Versions that the Client may, in its discretion, elect to implement, including PQRS reporting, E-Prescribing reporting and in becoming a "meaningful user."* c. *If Vendor is not in full compliance with any upcoming and future requirements mandated by CMS or other federal entity, and this results in the Client not being fully certified by applicable federal entities, and this leads to financial penalties on the Client's reimbursement revenue from governmental payers (Medicare, Tricare, Medicare Advantage, etc.), the amount of penalties suffered by the Client in a year will be deducted from the annual licensing fees to Vendor.*

Summary

Organizations must know and understand the contents of their third-party vendor contracts. This awareness is especially important considering increasing cyber-attacks. You have everything to lose if you don't take seriously the security vulnerabilities and risks caused by your vendor relationships. While this chapter provided several examples of negotiable terms, it is crucial to develop a list of all issues important to the organization to ensure nothing gets missed. Defining the problems and the desired outcomes will help you navigate this process. By completing this vital exercise, you will have much to gain, including peace of mind, if you protect your organization at the contract level.

Resources

1. Garnet, H. How to Review a Vendor Contract. March 4, 2020. https://www.ven minder.com/blog/how-review-vendor-contract. Accessed May 20, 2020.
2. Office of the National Coordinator for Health Information Technology. EHR Contracts Untangled: Selecting Wisely, Negotiating Terms, and Understanding the Fine Print. https://www.healthit.gov/sites/default/files/EHR_Contracts_Untangled.pdf. Accessed May 20, 2020.
3. HealthIT.gov. What are Important Items to Include in a Vendor Contract? Factors to Consider in Contract Negotiations. https://www.healthit.gov/faq/what-are-important-items-include-vendor-contract. Accessed May 20, 2020.
4. UpCounsel. Negotiating SaaS Agreements: Everything You Need to Know. https://www.upcounsel.com/negotiating-saas-agreements. Accessed May 20, 2020.
5. AAFP. Understanding EHR Contracting & Pricing. https://www.aafp.org/practice-management/health-it/product/contracting-pricing.html. Accessed May 20, 2020.
6. Overly, M.R. Drafting and Negotiating Effective Cloud Computing Agreements. *Lexis Practice Advisor Journal*, November 11, 2013. https://www.lexisnexis.com/lexis-practice-advisor/the-journal/b/lpa/posts/drafting-and-negotiating-effective-cloud-computing-agreements. Accessed May 20, 2020.
7. Pinson, S. Negotiating Contracts: 12 Key Terms to Negotiate in a Software as a Service or Cloud Service Agreement. *Lexology*, April 25, 2017. https://www.lexology.com/library/detail.aspx?g=8ed191ca-f24e-4919-9196-db5d7980b261. Accessed May 20, 2020.

Chapter 11

Implementation and Project Management

Implementing an EMR system is by no means an easy task. Typically, a successful implementation involves significant planning long before going live. There are many aspects of an implementation that can be overlooked, and without strict adherence to every detail, an implementation may result in a delay to "go live." Once the EMR is live, the work does not stop there. A post-go-live optimization period must be established internally to review lessons learned from go-live documented issues and enhancement tracking. In conjunction with the EMR system's metric reports, go-live issues should then be assessed and prioritized for resolution. The evolution of an EMR system post-go-live will require continuous alignment of the organization's long-term vision alongside the management of current state-integrated applications and downstream systems. The increased recognition of project management as an effective means of completing numerous and complex project efforts has spawned the creation of a program management office (PMO) within many large healthcare organizations. According to a 2017 Pulse of the Profession report by the Project Management Institute (PMI), "the percentage of organizations with a PMO continues an upward trend—from 61 percent in 2007 to 71 percent today."[1] The program management definition varies according to the source; however, the Project Management Institute (PMI) defines it as "a group of related projects managed in a coordinated manner to obtain benefits not available from managing them individually." They go on to say "effective program management provides a mechanism for controlling the strategic, financial and operational risks of major endeavors."

The primary goal of a PMO is to yield successful results from effectively standardizing project management processes, policies, reporting and communication methods. For the office to be most effective, it should reflect the organization's culture and overall vision and strategy.

Implementing a PMO

Most healthcare organizations have undergone a multitude of projects that did not end on time, went over budget, changed in project scope throughout the process and/or did not align with leadership's overall vision. Although many potential variables can derail projects, they typically fail due to the following reasons:

- Absence of a clear organizational vision or project objectives
- Lack of visibility of all projects and resource workload
- Insufficient communication

For these reasons, the creation of a PMO has become the latest trend in large healthcare organizations to help facilitate overall project success. Setting up a new organizational PMO can be arduous. When developed correctly, the PMO will serve as the central point of the organization, responsible for the methods and tools used to align and maintain the organization's vision.

When an organization sets up a PMO, it should keep it simple. The following are three steps and key questions to answer to begin the framework of your organization's PMO:

1. **Identify key stakeholders**. Having the right team from the start can make or break the PMO. Begin to discuss internally if the skill set is currently in-house, and what the expectations of each key stakeholder would entail. Describe the value benefits of the PMO; seek advice, incorporate suggestions and gain buy-in to the PMO concept. Below are some critical questions to ask:
   - Who will be the members of the PMO?
   - Who is the executive sponsor for the PMO initiative?
   - To whom does the PMO report?
   - Who reports to the PMO?
   - What areas/departments will be covered by the PMO?

2. **Define organizational vision and project objectives**. Establishing a clear and compelling vision is critical to project management. To ensure future success, it is imperative that the organization adequately define the overall goals, strategies and achievement factors. Once the leaders outline these key initiatives, the PMO can be leveraged to help prioritize, manage and execute these strategic initiatives. Here are a few essential questions to ask:
   - What is the business case for developing the PMO?
   - Where will the PMO fit within the organization?
   - What are the PMO's objectives to achieve short-, medium- and long-term goals?
   - How many projects will be managed or supported by the PMO?

3. **Establish PMO responsibilities**. Generally, the PMO is responsible for guidance, standardization, introducing and establishing clear processes and metrics related to the practices surrounding the management and implementation of projects within the organization. There is no standard approach to PMO development; however, an effective PMO has a solid foundation aligned with the organizational strategic initiatives. The PMO is responsible for providing accurate information to support effective decision-making. Table 11.1 gives a sample industry-standard checklist of a typical PMO's function and scope.

Figure 11.1 is a visual of a basic PMO framework, as described above.

See Figure 11.2 for the industry standard planning tool, PMO framework, for the progression of project management initiatives.

Establishing a PMO Framework

PMO frameworks can vary by the size and complexity of each organization. According to a 2013 PMI Pulse of Profession Report, there are five typical frameworks:[2]

■ **Organizational unit PMO/business unit PMO/divisional PMO/ departmental PMO**. Provides project-related services to support a business unit or division within an organization, including, but not limited to, portfolio management, governance, operational project support and human resources utilization.

Table 11.1 Standardization of Documentation and Project Management Tools to Support Projects

Task	Completed
• Project initiation 　• Project request document 　• Scope statement 　• Project classification	
• Planning 　• Communications matrix 　• Project schedule 　• Requirements checklist	
• Execution 　• Deliverables acceptance 　• Issues log 　• Meeting agenda/minutes 　• Project status report	
• Cost control 　• Amount of necessary resources 　• Logistics 　• Duration of the requirement for these resources 　• The size and scope of the project(s) 　• Funds to support the project	
• Risk and impact reports	
• Change management 　• Change management document 　• Change management governance approval	
• Closing 　• Lessons learned log 　• Project survey	
• Documentation 　• Network folder 　• Share point	
• Resource allocation management grid	
• Audits	
• Develop training curriculums	
• Mentoring of project team members	
• Managing impact of multiple ongoing projects	
• Establish "best practices"	

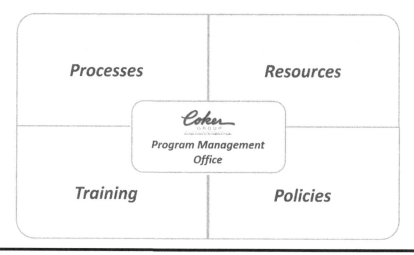

Figure 11.1   PMO frameworks (1). (©Coker Group 2019.)

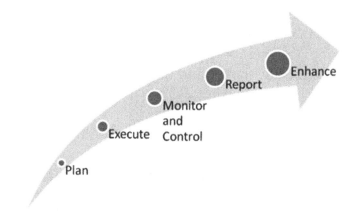

Figure 11.2   PMO frameworks (2). https://iiste.org/Journals/index.php/EJBM.

■ **Project-specific PMO/project office/program office**. Provides project-related services as a temporary entity established to support a specific project or program. May include supporting data management, coordination of governance and reporting, and administrative activities to support the project or program team.

■ **Project support/services/controls office or PMO**. Provides enabling processes to continuously support the management of project, program or portfolio work throughout the organization. Uses the governance, processes, practices and tools established by the organization, and provides administrative support for the delivery of the project, program or portfolio work within its domain.

- **Enterprise-/organization-wide/strategic/corporate/portfolio/ global PMO**. The highest-level PMO in organizations having one, this PMO is often responsible for the alignment of project and program work to corporate strategy, establishing and ensuring appropriate enterprise governance, and performing portfolio management functions to ensure strategy alignment and benefits realization. Center of Excellence/ Center of Competency Supports projects work by equipping the organization with methodologies, standards and tools to enable project managers to deliver projects better. Increases the capability of the organization through good practices and a central point of contact for project managers.

Even after the initiation of a project management office, there must be processes in place to manage projects. This initiative will allow leadership to focus on "managing" projects rather than having the challenging task of deciding which projects move forward and which ones do not. The goal of having a process in place is to be able to show priority levels for each project. Typically, they are in tiers, for example, Tier 1, Tier 2 and Tier 3.

- Tier 1 projects identify undertakings that are of high priority to the organization.
- Tier 2 projects identify necessary endeavors, but which are not a high priority. These projects will move forward, but only when resources are available.
- Tier 3 projects may still require added diligence, resources, funding or approval.

Having a process in place for moving projects forward is important when trying to manage projects effectively within the project management office. The process allows the projects to move forward quickly if all the fundamentals are in place to enable the initiative to move to Tier 1. The method also allows the employees and stakeholders to know where their projects rank with regards to the organization's overall goals and vision.

The positive results of the 2017 PMI Pulse of the Profession report suggest that more organizations recognize the strategic value of projects and programs – and that how well they support these strategic initiatives and the professionals who manage them matters to their long-term relevance and ultimate viability.[3]

Summary

The PMO has many roles and should evolve with industry standards as well as aligning with the organization's strategic goals and initiatives. The greatest impact that a PMO can supply is the ability to improve organizational alignment while providing transparency for organizational decision-makers. Standardizing projects from initiation to close has many benefits. For example, established processes and methods help optimize collaboration and minimize communication conflicts. The training that project managers undergo ensures that they apply experience and avoid known mistakes. PMOs can ensure that projects are run smoothly with the appropriate amount of resources and with the quick implementation of decisions. Building a PMO can be a proactive tactic that helps reduce cost overruns, delays and cancellations of projects. As operating budgets potentially decrease, no organization would complain about decreased costs and increased efficiency.

Resources

1. PMI 2017 Pulse of the Profession: Project Success Rates Climb, Fewer Dollars Wasted, Philadelphia, February 8, 2017. https://www.pmi.org/about/press-media/press-releases/pmi-2017-pulse-of-the-profession. Accessed January 5, 2020.
2. PMI 2013 Pulse of the Profession: PMO Frameworks, November 2013. https://www.pmi.org/-/media/pmi/documents/public/pdf/learning/thought-leadership/pulse/pmo-frameworks.pdf. Accessed January 5, 2020.
3. PMI's Pulse of the Profession, Transforming the High Cost of Low Performance: Success Rates Rise, 2017 9th Global Project Management Survey. https://www.pmi.org/-/media/pmi/documents/public/pdf/learning/thought-leadership/pulse/pulse-of-the-profession-2017.pdf. Accessed January 5, 2020.

Chapter 12

Future Healthcare Information Trends and the Internet of Things

As we look beyond EHR, the next generation of automation will mostly come from enhancing existing systems or will be device-driven. It is common to see information technology (IT) performance, including processing speed, double every two to five years. However, the healthcare industry has been slow to incorporate technology. The slow growth of EHR adoption is confirmed when considering that, after over two decades, we still lack full adoption. As technology continues to permeate healthcare operations, driving innovation, increasing efficiency and, most importantly, improving patient outcomes, we can expect to see more disruption. Thus, while it is important to stay grounded in the present and provide optimal care for patients now, it is also vital to look to the future to gain insight into how technology can move a hospital or practice forward.

This chapter will examine future trends ranging from budding technologies to trends in strategies that soon will reshape the healthcare landscape. As technology progresses, so do the instruments and technologies that are available to healthcare. Some technologies that will be instrumental in shaping the future of healthcare are discussed in previous chapters, such as the use of artificial intelligence (AI) in Chapter 5, and advanced analytics in Chapter 8. This chapter, Future Healthcare IT Trends and the Internet of Things, will serve to spotlight and examine the impact of technologies that may be less known.

The IT-Driven Remote Workforce Trends

At the time of writing this chapter, the COVID-19 pandemic has been spreading worldwide and affecting workflows. Little preparation prior to the rise of the pandemic was possible due to the rapid spread of the disease. This crisis has caused many organizations across the United States and the world to adapt aggressively to the changing climate. One of the primary deviations is the transition of employees to remote workers. While it may be too soon to call this a trend, this massive shift from on-premises to remote workers likely will reshape our approach to workforce management. The early indications seem to suggest that the approach has been an overall success.

During the COVID-19 pandemic, quarantine suggestions and mandates have occurred regularly. With people being confined to their own homes, the only potential replacement for the work that was done on premises is to transition those responsibilities to be completed from home for staff who can work remotely. Providing employees with the necessary equipment and technology to complete their duties from home decreases the level of disruption that results from the quarantine. Further, it can decrease overhead long-term.

Some employers have held negative perceptions of remote work in the past with most concerns around a loss in production per hours worked. However, recent studies have shown that remote work benefits both employers and employees. Airtasker completed a study of 1,004 full-time employees; 505 of the studied employees were remote employees, and recorded the following production numbers from their study published in *Business News Daily*:[1,2]

- Remote employees would take longer breaks than office employees (22 minutes on average compared to 18 minutes) but would work an additional 10 minutes per day on average.
- Remote employees work an additional 1.4 days per month than in-office employees. Over the course of the year, this added approximately 17 additional workdays per employee.
- Employees reported whether they felt like their employer was disrupting their workflow. In this study, 15% of remote workers reported that their employer did distract them compared to the 22% of on-site employees who also reported the distraction.
- On-site employees studied were unproductive for 37 minutes per day on average while remote employees were unproductive for only 27 minutes, both not including lunch or breaks.

■ Average total daily time discussing nonwork-related topics with co-workers for remote employees studied was 29 minutes compared to 66 minutes for on-site employees.

These statistics exemplify the potential benefits of leveraging a remote workforce for an employer. As mentioned, remote work can also benefit the employees who are working remotely. The same study, shown in Figure 12.1, found positive results for employees who work from home compared to averages for on-site employees.

Despite the positive benefits of working remotely for both the employer and employee, the study showed the remote employees had a higher likelihood to struggle finding a work–life balance (29% compared 23%, respectively). However, the American Psychological Association has advocated that, when implemented correctly, working remotely can increase employee satisfaction. It is important to have a firm structure in place when implementing a system for employees to work remotely.[3] Where does an employer start, and what should be implemented prior to utilizing remote work for employees? Table 12.1 (A Basic Framework for Implementing a Remote Workforce) is a list of actionable items to consider when establishing a remote workforce.

After the COVID-19 pandemic subsides, it is reasonable to expect that many positions that have shifted to remote employees have the potential to remain remote. Transitioning positions to remote employees can reduce overhead for an organization as less workspace is required to staff the same

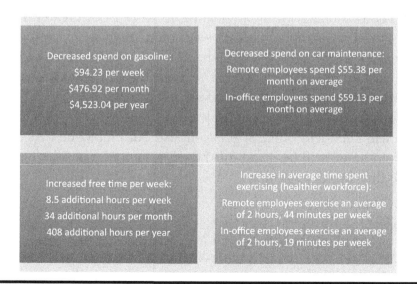

Figure 12.1   Benefits of working remotely vs on-site.

Table 12.1   A Basic Framework for Implementing a Remote Workforce

Policy and procedure	Similar to any policies and procedures that would be in place for on-site employees, it is essential to develop policies and procedures and establish guidelines regarding remote employees. More than likely these already exist in most organizations and would just need to be adapted for remote employees.
Current capabilities vs necessary capabilities	Determine current state vs what the desired future state is for the organization. Most remote work will require hardware for the remote employees to complete and could potentially require additional software capabilities. Perform an analysis to determine what the needs will be for the organization.
Cyber and patient security	Remote access can increase risk when implemented improperly. Home networks, lack of auto-sleep functions on computers and improperly managed patient information can all be forms of risk that are created. Perform a risk analysis and identify additional holes in security that would need to be filled. This can also be addressed with policies and procedures.
Promoting a healthy work–life balance	Remote employees typically suffer from a struggle find a healthy work–life balance. Working from home brings the workspace into the same space in which an individual is living and interacting with family members and friends. Intervention from management, such as promoting social interactions between employees or implementing working hours guidelines, can help employees maintain a health work–life balance.

positions. The potential for remote healthcare work is far greater than what is currently used. In many organizations, remote employees can be leveraged for positions such as account managers, patient-education or case advocates, scribes and some revenue cycle management positions.

Finally, moving the workforce to off-site offices will also alter the real estate landscape and our approach to leasing office space. If this trend continues, we will need less office space to house our employees. As a bonus, working from home will be good for the environment, considering that it will reduce the carbon footprint.

Predictions

A shift in the workforce from on-premises to remote is likely to instigate some "big brother" types of innovation for tracking employee productivity and activities. Outlook, for example, already has tools that can report back to employers on how much time an individual is spending responding to e-mail. Computers can call home to let employers know when activity starts and stops. Protecting employee and patient privacy from a home network intrusion will become a priority for companies that allow their employees to work from home. Employee manuals and policies will also have to be revised. One major stipulation will be employees accepting eDiscovery on their personal home networks/devices in the event of a breach or an audit. So, while there are many benefits, there are also tradeoffs and risks that will result in more innovation to address.

Telehealth Trends

Although Chapter 7 addresses telehealth and EHRs, we will briefly cover it here in the context of current and future trends. Prior to the COVID-19 crisis, telehealth was working its way into the market as an up-and-coming alternative to the traditional in-office visit. The growth of telehealth has rapidly increased during the pandemic and has provided a route for patients to consult with their physicians in compliance with quarantine guidelines. Following COVID-19, telehealth will not only be available to patients, but could also reasonably become the prevailing pattern for many traditional visits. The possibility of telehealth replacing all in-office visits is minimal with the current technology that is available for both patients and providers. However, the COVID-19 pandemic has taught the healthcare market that telehealth is a viable solution to providing patient care, and it can alleviate traffic for providers in an already congested system. The illustration in Figure 12.2 may represent a typical physician's side of a telehealth patient encounter.

The growth of telehealth will rely on many factors. These factors include the ability to record vitals remotely, technological capabilities for providers and patients, reimbursement development and the acceptance of telehealth as a form of communication by both providers and patients. Technological innovations have already been made to provide care remotely. Patients can record many vitals from home and report them to their care provider. As an example, smart watches and other wearables have gained traction and typically can monitor heart rates and other vitals and transmit them to the patient's phone. Additionally, many households will have a scale where individuals can monitor their own weight. Currently, the gap in the market is the access to other technologies that can broaden the scope of telehealth. The growth of wearables and other at-home resources for recording health will further advance the role of telehealth in the marketplace.

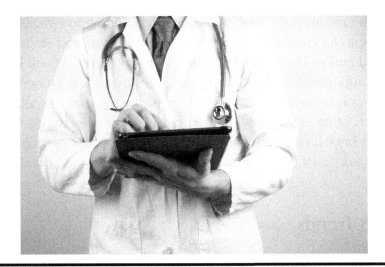

Figure 12.2   Telehealth from the provider side.

Regulations regarding restrictions on providing telehealth have been relaxed to an extent during the COVID-19 crisis. Patient privacy (HIPAA) mandates are still in effect during the crisis, but loosened restrictions have made it easier for organizations to provide care to their patients. The crisis has proven to the public and industry leaders that telehealth can and will be a staple for providing care in the future.

Telehealth by the Numbers

According to MarketWatch, the global telehealth market was valued at USD 2.68 billion in 2016 and is projected to reach USD 22.71 billion by 2025, growing at a CAGR of 26.8% from 2016 to 2025.[4]

Another way to predict trends is to follow the money. When spending is increasing year over year and continues to grow, it is a solid indicator that the market is responding favorably. This assumption is supported by Adroit Market Research, which tracked telemedicine revenue over a ten-year period (see Figure 12.3).[5]

The other indicator is consumer reaction. In a recent survey conducted by Harris Poll/Xerox found patients had a very favorable opinion of telehealth.[6] Figure 12.4 indicates the benefits that consumers found most appealing.

Predictions

Telehealth will continue to evolve and become more robust. Some have even suggested that the hospital bed of the future may be in your home

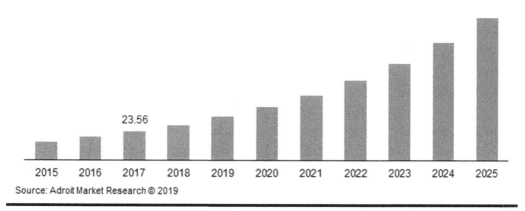

Global Telemedicine Market Revenue, 2018-2025 (USD Billion)

23.56

2015 2016 2017 2018 2019 2020 2021 2022 2023 2024 2025

Source: Adroit Market Research © 2019

Figure 12.3   Global telemedicine market revenue, 2018–2025 (USD billion).

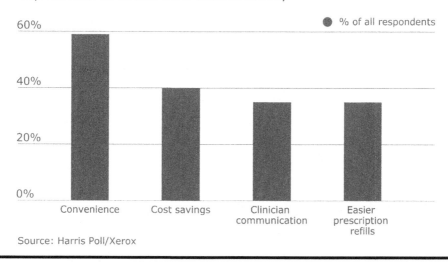

Telehealth connects with consumers

Top benefits of virtual care cited in survey

● % of all respondents

60%

40%

20%

0%

Convenience   Cost savings   Clinician   Easier
communication   prescription
refills

Source: Harris Poll/Xerox

Figure 12.4   Telehealth connects with consumers – top benefits of virtual care cited in survey.

for chronic and low-risk conditions. A more plausible prediction will be the integration of devices and wearables into the telehealth platforms. For example, an Apple Watch can track movement. If a provider is treating a patient with behavioral health issues, and there are no signs of movement, someone could intervene to check on the patient. Other wireless devices can track oxygen levels, heart rates and blood pressure and send back alerts if the patient needs attention.

Infection Control Technology Trends

The Centers for Disease Control and Prevention (CDC) reports that 1 in 31 U.S. patients will suffer from at least one infection in association with their hospital care.[7] While considerable progress with healthcare-associated infections (HAI) has been made, the additional adoption of budding technologies can continue to improve these metrics and improve patient safety. Current and future technologies will continue to improve metrics through added sanitization and by using artificial intelligence (AI) to provide updates to providers for something as simple as hand washing. An emerging technology in the infection control space is the use of ultraviolet (UV) light to kill viruses and bacteria. UVC Cleaning Systems Inc. report that their current UV systems are 99.999% effective up to 16 ft.[8] The use of UV light in care settings reduces sanitation time and resources required, and can improve sanitation standards across an organization. See Figure 12.5 for a photo of the UV light.

In a CDC-funded study underway at Emory University Hospital Midtown (EUHM) and Emory Johns Creek Hospital (EJCH), researchers are testing an

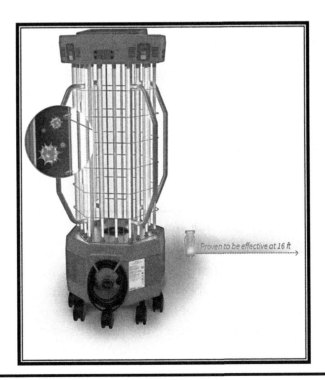

Figure 12.5   UVC Cleaning Systems UV light.

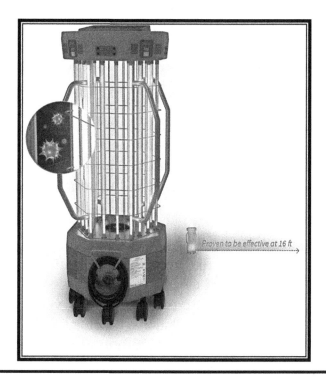

Proven to be effective at 16 ft

Figure 12.6   Electronic sensors to detect hand sanitization.

AI monitoring system to measure hand hygiene compliance. Data are collected by electronic sensors attached to alcohol hand-rub and soap dispensers in patient rooms and hallways. These sensors (see Figure 12.6) know when a caregiver enters a patient care area and will sound an alarm if they exit the area without washing their hands and/or if they enter an area having not washed their hands after leaving the prior area.

Technologies that monitor hand sanitization may seem redundant to some. However, if the risk of HAIs can still decline, any progress toward creating a safer environment for patient care is in the best interest of the patient. The further advancement and adoption of technologies that monitor and improve sanitation will create better outcomes and improve metrics.

Predictions

The COVID-19 crisis will drive demand for this type of innovation, and it will extend beyond hospitals. The food and beverage and hospitality industries will explore ways to reduce infections. Hotels will start promoting their rooms as fully disinfected after each stay. There likely will be thermal temperature-taking sensors at entrances to sporting events and concerts.

Artificial Intelligence (AI) Trends

The use of artificial intelligence in healthcare was highlighted earlier in Chapter 5. AI is a future trend in healthcare due to the low adoption rates of this technology across the industry. Healthcare organizations today have access to more data than ever before in human history. Specifically, technology users generate 2.5 quintillion bytes of data each day, according to Forbes.[9] AI provides the ability to categorize and learn from the data that users are creating to generate efficiencies in the treatment process. These efficiencies are not limited to patient care and will also extend to the efficiency of organizations. The improvements in the process for organizations have the potential to alleviate the pressures of an ongoing healthcare staffing shortage in the U.S., as well as the ability to improve the financial position of organizations through several means.

Artificial intelligence is still not a perfect technology. As discussed earlier in this book, AI can deliver many solutions, but it is still navigating many issues for patients and providers. Staying informed on the technology will ensure that an organization is using the most current tools available, while also adhering to the ethical requirements that AI imposes.

The future of AI depends on massive quantities of quality data to predict an outcome. All AI systems start with an input layer, which is where the information is ingested. The information then gets processed in hidden layers that are based on statistics and logic. For example, if the input layer identifies the patient as female, the hidden layer will narrow down the possibilities to only outcomes that are applicable to a female patient. The next layers would be added data points to further predict the desired outcome. Adding information such as the patient's age, family history and current conditions would act as additional filters to narrow the outcome. The AI might also have the aid of a chat-bot in real time to deal with variances. Figure 12.7 (also presented in Chapter 5) is an illustration of the how AI logic processes data.

Input = ingesting data
Hidden layers = processing the data
Output = the answer/decision

Predictions

AI holds the potential to become one of the most disruptive innovations of all the trends we have discussed. It is hard to say where it will go as

INPUT
LAYER   HIDDEN
LAYERS   OUTPUT
LAYER

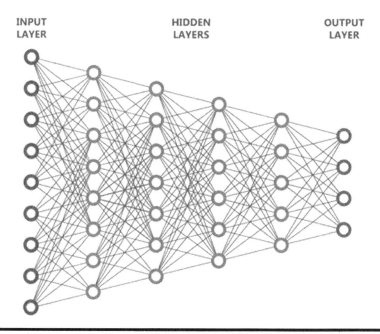

Figure 12.7   How artificial intelligence processes data.

the possibilities are endless, but we predict it will first target tasks that are repeatable and predictable. We now see vendors using AI to alert providers to drug-to-drug interaction. It has become immensely popular in preventing denials as it can look at a claim and immediately determine if the coding is correct for the charge.

Before a provider renders services, AI can tell which patients have the propensity to pay on time. While the use of AI for medical decision-making is also controversial, we predict it will eventually be capable of making a diagnosis for conditions that have very predictable and undisputed clinical markers.

Blockchain in Healthcare Trends

Blockchain has a wide array of applications across industries. In healthcare, blockchain can have an impact by securing the transfer of patient medical records, managing the supply chain and helping healthcare researchers unlock genetic codes.[10] Blockchain has the potential to record clinical trials in real time which supplies more comprehensive and accurate data while transmitting the data securely. Before we can understand the benefits of blockchain, we must first understand what it is.

Blockchain is a log of activity that is time-stamped, tamper-proof and shared across a network of computers. Each transaction that goes into the log of activity is enclosed in a block and linked together in chronological order to form a chain, giving it the name blockchain. Blockchain is a shared record of transactions that enables participants to share data with each other securely. The blockchain cuts out the middleman that is involved in most processes and tracks what was exchanged and when the exchange occurred. An example provided by modern healthcare is that if one insurance company in an alliance calls a doctor's office to verify an address and updates that information in a blockchain system of records, then all members of the alliance would see the change in real time.[11] This feature would eliminate additional work for all alliance members to update the same information as well as decreasing the amount of work that is required by the doctor's office to update all of the alliance members.

This technology has been available for about a decade but has only become more widespread in recent years. Where blockchain provides the most benefit is in areas where redundancies are abundant and different sets of data must be reconciled. Information is stored across multiple devices rather than storing data and information on a single computer, which can be easily corrupted. Blockchain can provide benefits in multiple areas of the industry:

- Physician credentialing
- Pharmaceutical clinical trials
- Avoiding fraud
- Cybersecurity
- Billing
- Claim tracking across the entire life cycle
- Registration
- Insurance verification
- Accessing patient information/creating a more portable patient health record
- Provider directory information
- Communication between organizations

Predictions

As with AI, large quantities of quality data are needed. We predict there will be a race for the monetization of these data. Companies will start to aggregate and sell the data with the owner's permission. A marketplace for the data is already in place for the public good. An immediate example is with researchers in responding to viruses, as with the COVID-19 response. Monetizing data is an important step to entice the stakeholders and investors. Blockchain technology for healthcare is still in its infancy and does not currently possess many of the capabilities discussed here. Currently, blockchain is not used to store or transmit sensitive patient data. Ideally, in the future, blockchain will provide all the benefits we have presented – and more. However, we will need to see additional growth, funding and development to support many of the functions that the healthcare industry requires of the technology. The goal of blockchain in healthcare should be to create a comprehensive and portable patient record that connects all the dispersed pieces in a patient's health history. Figure 12.8 illustrates how blockchain works.

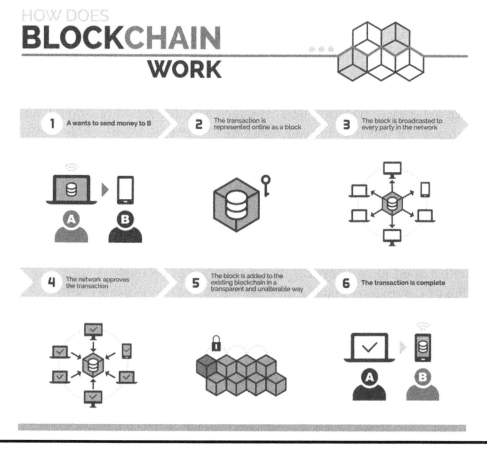

Figure 12.8   How blockchain works. Source: www.coinmama.com/guide/what-is-the-blockchain.

The Internet of Things (IoT) Trends

The Internet of things (IoT) is the latest catch-all term for anything connected to the Internet without an operating system. It is a network of physical devices that uses connectivity to enable the exchange of data. IoT encapsulates a wide array of physical devices, from healthcare-specific devices, such as biosensors or X-ray machines, to wearable devices that exist in the consumer marketplace. Today, many physical objects and devices have embedded sensors, actuators, software and network connectivity that are linked to capture and exchange information. These devices can sense their environment and transfer data to tools that can understand the complexity of the large volumes of data and respond swiftly and provide solutions. In healthcare, providers can access data that are tracked in real time to determine treatment plans and track vitals. Previously, providers would have relied on a smaller data set collected in the office or from a patient testimonial based on the individual's tracking of their data, which has a greater potential for providing inaccurate information.

Current challenges facing the use of IoT-enabled devices revolve around their interoperability with EHR systems, the cost of integrating the data created with EHR systems, a lack of software development and patient and physician acceptance of receiving big data from these devices. Gradually, acceptance of IoT-enabled devices has increased. The increased utilization of Apple Watch and other smart watch technology is a prime example. More people are now wearing devices regularly that can track heart rate, provide irregular rhythm notifications, detect a fall by the patient and record an electrocardiogram (ECG).

The following is a list of IoT uses and examples:

- Continuously monitor chronic diseases
- Track patients through a facility
- Pill-shaped micro cameras that a patient can swallow
- Smart continuous glucose monitoring (CGM) and insulin pens
- Connected inhalers
- Coagulation testing
- Connected contact lenses

IOT Concerns and Risk

Beyond the compromising of personal data, IoT devices have the potential to harm a patient seriously. An early national spotlight on this fear was former Vice President Dick Cheney's request that the wireless capabilities of his pacemaker be disabled due to fear of hacking.[12] Johnson & Johnson has issued a warning that their insulin pumps were susceptible to cyber hacking attacks, causing overdosing.

The U.S. Food and Drug Administration (FDA), along with the Department of Homeland Security (DHS), in an effort to counter these risks, published guidelines for establishing end-to-end security for connected medical devices. These guidelines are available at www.fda.gov/medical-devices/digital-health/cybersecurity.

Summary

It is imperative for hospitals and medical practices to take advantage of the ever-improving features offered by modern technology and to begin looking beyond EHR. Everything from cloud computing, to telemedicine services, to IoT utilization should be up for consideration. However, as healthcare organizations implement more technology, it is critical for cyber risks and cybersecurity to be a top priority and concern. Implementing innovative solutions should be in harmony with a holistic cybersecurity plan, regulatory compliance and patient safety. Demonstrating the ability to improve healthcare outcomes and increased patient satisfaction will be the key to staying viable as we transition to value-based medicine. The dependency on quality data will be enormous and detrimental to those who are not prepared and/or lack the tools necessary to be competitive.

Resources

1. Airtasker. The Benefits of Working from Home: Comparing the Productivity, Spending and Health of Remote vs. In-Office Employees, March 21, 2020. https://www.airtasker.com/blog/the-benefits-of-working-from-home/. Accessed May 13, 2020.
2. Peek, Sean. Communication Technology and Inclusion Will Shape the Future of Remote Work. *Business News Daily*, March 18, 2020. https://www.businessnewsdaily.com/8156-future-of-remote-work.html. Accessed May 13, 2020.
3. Greenbaum, Zara. The Future of Remote Work. *American Psychological Association*, October 21, 2019. https://www.apa.org/monitor/2019/10/cover-remote-work. Accessed May 13, 2019.

4. Press Release: Telehealth Market Projections and Future Opportunities Recorded for the Period Until 2025. *Market Watch*, March 23, 2020. https://www.marketwatch.com/press-release/telehealth-market-projections-and-future-opportunities-recorded-for-the-period-until-2025-2020-03-23. Accessed May 14, 2020.

5. Global Telemedicine Market Size by End Users (Telehospitals/Teleclinics and Telehome); by Component (Services, Hardware, Software, Telecom and Networking); by Region and Forecast 2018 to 2025. *Adroit Market Research*. https://www.adroitmarketresearch.com/industry-reports/telemedicine-market. Accessed May 14, 2020.

6. Albinus, Phil. Telemedicine Still Faces Roadblocks Despite Employee Enthusiasm. *Employee Benefit Adviser*, March 01, 2018, https://www.employeebenefitadviser.com/news/telemedicine-still-faces-roadblocks-despite-employee-enthusiasm. Accessed May 14, 2020.

7. 2018 National and State Healthcare-Associated Infections Progress Report. Centers for Disease Control and Prevention, Undated. https://www.ded.gov/hai/data/portal/progress-report.html. Accessed May 14, 2020.

8. UVC Disinfection Machine for Lease or Purchase in Michigan - UVC Cleaning Systems, Inc. https://www.uvccleaningsystems.com/. Accessed May 14, 2020.

9. Marr, Bernard. How Much Data Do We Create Every Day? The Mind-Blowing Stats Everyone Should Read. *Forbes*, May 21, 2018. https://www.forbes.com/sites/bernardmarr/2018/05/21/how-much-data-do-we-create-every-day-the-mind-blowing-stats-everyone-should-read/#3d39bd7e60ba. Accessed May 14, 2020.

10. Daly, Sam. 15 Examples of How Blockchain is Reviving Healthcare. *Built In*, March 25, 2020. https://builtin.com/blockchain/blockchain-healthcare-applications-companies. Accessed May 14, 2020.

11. Livingston, Shelby. Will Blockchain Save the Healthcare System? *Modern Healthcare*, February 09, 2019. https://www.modernhealthcare.com/article/20190209/TRANSFORMATION02/190209953/will-blockchain-save-the-healthcare-system. Accessed May 14, 2020.

12. Franzen, Carl. Dick Cheney Had the Wireless Disabled on His Pacemaker to Avoid Risk of Terrorist Tampering, October 21, 2013. https://abcnews.go.com/US/vice-president-dick-cheney-feared-pacemaker-hacking/story?id=20621434.

Chapter 13

Chapter 13

Tools and Policies

This chapter is a collection of resources and tools used in actual EHR selection and implementation projects. These tools are intended to be guidelines, templates and examples of proven resources and policies, but they may need to be modified to meet the needs of your practice.

Project management policies and tools
Project staffing models, including sample job descriptions and recruiting tools
Readiness assessment tool
Vendor vetting tools
Sample RFI
Sample RFP
Sample demo scripts
Sample scorecards
Sample site visit checklist
Sample list of reference questions
ROI calculator
Stimulus payout schedules

Project Management Policies and Tools

Project management is more than a set of disciplines and principles that support an efficient way of managing an EHR project. Project management is a team effort that has its base in traditional management theory but has developed its own system of tools and techniques.

The need for a consistent set of tools and policies stems from the desire to have the ability to view real-time project status to ensure your project is staying on budget and on course. These policies and tools detail the processes, workflows and procedures related to proven EHR adoption techniques. The purpose is to serve as a reference guide for the project leadership.

Project resources include financial support, leadership, and management as well as dedicated staff time for project implementation. Typically, project budgets are created when the decision to implement a project is made. A common pitfall in project development is not budgeting enough personnel for the project and making the project an additional responsibility for those already in place by job description. For example, an EHR project needs the following personnel with dedicated project time:

- physician/provider champion
- project manager
- IT manager
- EHR application specialist
- trainers
- "super users"

Step One – Define Roles and Responsibilities

- **Physician or executive sponsor.** This position is the most senior level of management and holds other project members accountable for the deliverables of a project. The physician/executive sponsor signs off on project initiation and closure. This individual receives information on project status from the project managers (progress to date, on time, on budget, critical issues, etc.) and in return makes budget and resource decisions.
- **Project manager.** Usually, this person is an experienced office leader, such as a nurse manager or team leader, who can own the project plan, assign resources, request and review weekly status reports (accomplishments, upcoming deliverables, issues, actual vs baseline, etc.) and maintain the project plans (create baseline, ensure posting of actual

work, prepare reports, etc.). The project manager approves or declines updates made by the resources and is responsible for reporting the project status to the physician/executive sponsor and for managing the work performed by the resources. (Note: Typically, it is best to select someone other than the office manager or administrator as the project manager. Usually, the office manager/administrator is busy managing the practice. He or she will find devoting the required time to project management to be challenging.)

■ **Project team members**. The project team are individuals who perform work assigned to them by the project manager. Team members are responsible for reporting back to the project manager on the status of the tasks assigned to them (current tasks as well as tasks that they will be working on in the future). In addition, it is the responsibility of the team members to report to the project managers whenever specific issues with the project arise. They also may be assigned the task of resolving the issues specific to their tasks.

Step Two – Organize Processes and Tasks

Organizing processes should be defined into five major categories:

1. **Initiate**. Building a formal process to handle project requests is a vital step towards eliminating unrealistic workloads and ad hoc resource assignments. For example, a user may request some customization to the EHR system that could result in exceeding the budget or the use of unallocated resources. The ability to decide which requests will become projects begins with understanding the definition of a project: *A project is a temporary endeavor with a beginning and an end, creates a unique product or service and has interrelated activities.*

2. **Analyze**. During the analyzing phase, the project stakeholders and team members gather the information that supports the planning phase, and, if necessary, the development or budget requirements necessary to support the project. A rule of thumb is to take the vendor's budget for their services and match it for what would be required in terms of time and resources needed on the practice side of the project. If the vendor projects they will need to devote 100 hours, you should expect to do the same because someone will have to be managing the vendor's activities.

3. **The plan**. The planning phase of the project allows the project manager to define manageable (and measurable) pieces of work and to organize

them into a schedule. To plan realistically for the project, it is important to identify dependencies on external requirements. For example, the milestone for staff training is predicated on having the training room set up. Setting up the training workstations would be predicated on locating a training room with enough space and power supplies. While this may seem basic, a good project plan must consider dependencies and have someone responsible for making sure everything is in its right order or sequence. Finding out your training room does not have adequate power supply on the day of training would be very disruptive.

4. **Ways to execute**. All the analyses, information gathering and planning now must be put into motion. This phase of the project management lifecycle should include an industry-known process called design, build, test and implement (DBTI).

   a. **Design** what you want to accomplish. This can be done on a white board or by undertaking workflow mapping to understand how you want the EHR to respond to end-users.
   b. **Build** what you design.
   c. **Test** what you design and modify accordingly.
   d. **Implement** what you test once it is proven to work.

      Following the DBTI method as a tool to execute your EHR will give you the opportunity to ensure your methods are working before you put the system into a live environment. Even after implementation, DBTI should be a standard policy for implementing new features or trying new methods of use.

5. **Transition**. Every project must have a start and an end. A clear-cut end to a project serves several purposes, including a well-defined transition into post-go-live and serves as a way to give ownership of the EHR to the end-users. The goals of the transition should include the following:

   a. Close out the project plan.
   b. Summarize the final project status. (There could be a few lingering issues that will require follow-up, but there should always be an official end to the project; otherwise, they can linger on forever.)
   c. Review lessons learned.
   d. Recognize the accomplishments of the team.
   e. Celebrate.

The key to any successful project is to have fun and to be reasonable. It is okay to experiment and to test your ideal. Many decisions will have to be made with incomplete information and through trial and error. Seek outside help, when possible, from those who have been through this process. You may even want to consider engaging an outside expert who has experience and knowledge with these types of projects. The role of the consultant should be to transfer knowledge and to support your decisions. They can also act as an objective third party, which is helpful for change management. You may also want to consider getting your project team members matching tee-shirts to give them the feeling of being on a team. Make sure they have a good workroom and allow for some rest. Burnout is common, so make sure team members have the opportunity to have some diversity in their roles and responsibilities. The planning tool given in Table 13.1 will serve as a sample for accomplishing your project.

Project Staffing Models

Staffing is critical for a successful implementation. Thus, the project team should be staffed appropriately with full-time, dedicated resources who are available for the meetings, training and conference calls. Upper-level management should immediately respond to staffing requirements, and no project should move forward without proper staffing.

A good idea of the workforce needed to support an EHR implementation, according to "Characterizing the Health Information Technology Workforce: Analysis from the HIMSS Analytics Database, April 2008," is as follows:

Job Description	Percentage
Project management	1%
Management	11%
Programmers	29%
Operations	8%
Network administration	9%
Help desk	8%
PC support	11%
Security	1%
Other	22%

Source: "IT Staffing Models from HIMSS Analytics April 2008 Database, April 17, 2008."

Table 13.1   Sample Project Plan

Task	Start	Finish	Resource
Sign contract			Client and vendor
Project manager assigned			Client and vendor
Mail implementation start-up guide			Vendor
Mail application manuals			Vendor
Project manager contacts customer			Vendor
Ship software			Vendor
Confirm receipt			Client
Project Planning			
Schedule pre-implementation meeting			Project manager and vendor
Pre-implementation meeting			Project manager and vendor
Project plan and timeline			Project manager
Approval of project plan and timeline			Project manager and project sponsor
Assigns responsible managers, employees			Project manager and project sponsor
Complete implementation start-up guide			Client
Customer information sheet			Client
Client information			Client
Site location			Client
Training questionnaire			Client
Travel information			Client
Telephone specifications			Client
Electrical specifications			Client
Cable specifications			Client
Existing computer equipment			Client

(Contiued)

Table 13.1 (Continued)   Sample Project Plan

Task	Start	Finish	Resource
Lab interface specification(s) form			Client
Billable service			Client
E-mail profile form			Client
Employee listing			Client
Manual form			Client
Site Preparation and Installation			
Schedule installation			Project manager
Install cabling			Client
Confirm location for workstations, servers			Client
Install communications lines			Client
Complete telephone specifications form			Client
Complete electrical specifications form			Client
Complete cable specifications form			Client
Complete existing computer equipment form(s)			Client
Complete e-mail profile form			Client
Identify fax server			Client
Identify dedicated fax line			Client
Identify/purchase modem			Client
Identify scanner need			Client
Identify printer need			Client
Installation			
Prepare network servers			IT support, client
Train client on installation steps			IT support, client
Install SQL server			IT support, client

(*Contiued*)

Table 13.1 (Continued)   Sample Project Plan

Task	Start	Finish	Resource
Install EHR database			IT support, client
Install PM database (if applicable)			IT support, client
Install client EPM and EHRS software			IT support, client
Install patient education			IT support, client
Install fax manager			IT support, client
Installation of dial-in access/RAS/ PCAnywhere® connection			IT support, client
Test installation			
Verify installation/access to all modules			Technical support, project manager, client
Confirm availability of all requested DB (at least production and test)			Technical support, project manager, client
Verify version of EHR installed			Technical support, project manager, client
Confirm documents available			Technical support, project manager, client
Confirm images available			Technical support, project manager, client
Confirm patient education installed			Technical support, project manager, client
Confirm fax manager installed			Technical support, project manager, client
Confirm crystal reports installed			Technical support, project manager, client
Confirm set DB installed			Technical support, project manager, client
Confirm e-mail access			Technical support, project manager, client
Confirm latest medication update run			Technical support, project manager, client

(Contiued)

Table 13.1 (Continued)   Sample Project Plan

Task	Start	Finish	Resource
Confirm CPT/ICD code availability			Technical support, project manager, client
Confirm access to client's system (Dial-in access/RAS/PCAnywhere®)			Technical support, project manager, client
Review post-installation issues			Technical support, project manager, client
Schedule follow-up (if necessary)			Project manager, client
Complete visit report and obtain client signature			Technical support, client
Interfaces			
EPM-EHR interface			
Install interface in test environment			
Schedule installation of EHR interface			Project manager
Transfer table data from EHR			Interface department
Inform PM interface ready for testing			Interface department
Confirm patient demographic data in EHR			Client, project manager
Confirm appointment schedules			Client, project manager
Confirm charge posting to PMS			Client, project manager
Interface transferred to production environment			
Schedule transfer of EHR interface			Project manager
Change billing interface environment			Interface department
Transfer table data from PM to EHR			Interface department

(*Contiued*)

Table 13.1 (Continued)   Sample Project Plan

Task	Start	Finish	Resource
Inform PM interface transfer complete			Interface department
Confirm patient demographic data			Client, project manager
Confirm appointment schedule			Client, project manager
Confirm charge posting to PM			Client, project manager
Steps necessary for any new lab interface			
Receive specification form/ information			Project coordinator
Forward copy of forms to interface dept			Project manager
Contact lab vendor for their specifications			Interface dept
Assign programmer to development			Interface dept
Determine communication link between client and lab vendor			Interface dept, third-party vendor
Communication with vendor programmer (on-going)			Interface dept
Test interface using vendor sample files			Interface dept
Alert PM interface ready for installation			Interface dept
Installation of lab interface in test environment			
Schedule installation of lab vendor interface			Project manager
Schedule installation with lab vendor			Interface dept
Install lab vendor interface			Interface dept, third-party vendor

(*Contiued*)

Table 13.1 (Continued) Sample Project Plan

Task	Start	Finish	Resource
Install communication link/tool			Interface dept
Alert PM interface installed and ready for testing			Interface dept, project manager
Train client on use of communication link/Rosetta interface			Interface dept, project manager
Confirm lab order processed by interface			Client, project manager
Confirm lab order received properly by lab vendor			Client, project manager
Confirm lab results received properly by client			Client, project manager
Lab interface transferred to production environment			
Schedule transfer of lab vendor interface			Project manager
Schedule transfer with lab vendor			Interface dept
Change lab vendor interface environment (client)			Interface dept
Change lab vendor interface environment (lab vendor)			Third-party vendor
Change communication link/ tool environment			Interface dept
Alert PM of complete transfer of environment to production			Interface dept
Confirm lab order processed by interface			Client, project manager
Confirm lab order received properly by lab vendor			Client, project manager
Confirm lab results received properly by EHR vendor			Client, project manager

(Contiued)

Table 13.1 (Continued)   Sample Project Plan

Task	Start	Finish	Resource
Preparation for on-Site			
Determine training site			Client
Determine training date			Client, project manager
Determine attendees for various training sessions			Client, project manager
Class content and documentation			Project manager
EHR Development Training			
EHR initial training (development)			Project manager, implementation specialist
System administration			Implementation specialist, client
Medical records module/client			Implementation specialist
Patient education			Implementation specialist, client
Table maintenance			Implementation specialist, client
Offline document generator			Implementation specialist, client
Lab assign			Implementation specialist, client
Template editor			Implementation specialist, client
Region editor			Implementation specialist, client
Template import/export			Implementation specialist, client
Document builder			Implementation specialist, client
Document import/export			Implementation specialist, client

(Contiued)

Table 13.1 (Continued)   Sample Project Plan

Task	Start	Finish	Resource
Discuss DB review process			Implementation specialist
Review status of application training			Implementation specialist, client
Verify client has contacted lab vendor for lab test codes			Implementation specialist
Complete visit report and obtain client signature			Implementation specialist
EHR Database Review, Modifications, Development			
Modify templates/documents			Implementation specialist, client
Modify crystal run lab template			Implementation specialist, client
Modify crystal run telephone call template			Client, implementation specialist
Test modified templates/documents			Implementation specialist, client
Phase 1 templates complete			Client, implementation specialist
System administration			Client
Gather employee access list			Client
Add users/assign rights			Client
Create groups/assign rights			Client
Table maintenance			Client
Review/add allergies			Client
Create diagnosis categories			Client
Add employers			Client
Add image descriptions			Client
Add lab components			Client

(Contiued)

Table 13.1 (Continued)   Sample Project Plan

Task	Start	Finish	Resource
Add lab groups			Client
Add lab tests			Client
Add languages			Client
Review/add medications			Client
Create medication groups			Client
Create modifiers categories			Client
Assign categories to providers			Client
Add pharmacies			Client
Add recall type/reason			Client
Review/add sig codes			Client
Add/review specialty			Client
Create Svc categories			Client
Add zip code			Client
Add zone			Client
Prescription report			
Forward copy of RX prescription			Client
Forward copies of other reports			Client
Create medication prescription report			Implementation specialist
Install medication prescription report			Implementation specialist
Test medication prescription report			Implementation specialist, client
Review medication prescription report			Client
Modify medication prescription report			Implementation specialist
Final approval on medication prescription report			Client

(Contiued)

Table 13.1 (Continued) Sample Project Plan

Task	Start	Finish	Resource
EHR Preparation of Production Database			
Schedule copy of test DB to production			Project manager
Copy test DB to production DB			Customer support
Alert PM copy is complete			Customer support
Confirm copy			Project manager, implementation specialist, client
Confirm production DB readiness			Project manager, implementation specialist, client
Confirm templates available and performing correctly			Project manager, implementation specialist, client
Confirm documents available and performing correctly			Project manager, implementation specialist, client
Confirm images available and performing correctly			Project manager, implementation specialist, client
Confirm providers available			Project manager, implementation specialist, client
Confirm locations available			Project manager, implementation specialist, client
Confirm appointments available			Project manager, implementation specialist, client
Confirm e-mail functioning			Project manager, implementation specialist, client

(Contiued)

Table 13.1 (Continued)   Sample Project Plan

Task	Start	Finish	Resource
Confirm ability to print documents and reports			Project manager, implementation specialist, client
Confirm ability to fax documents and reports			Project manager, implementation specialist, client
Set location of medication prescription report			Project manager, implementation specialist, client
Confirm ability to view medication report			Project manager, implementation specialist, client
Confirm ability to print medication report			Project manager, implementation specialist, client
Confirm ability to fax medication report			Project manager, implementation specialist, client
Confirm ability to order labs			Project manager, implementation specialist, client
Confirm ability to receive results			Project manager, implementation specialist, client
EHR Training			
Key user training			Project manager, implementation specialist
End user training			Project manager, implementation specialist, client
Go-live			Project manager, implementation specialist, client

EHR Readiness Assessment Tools

Readiness assessment tools come in a variety of structures and forms. The main purpose of an assessment tool is to gather the information necessary to determine how well the practice is prepared to adopt an EHR. The sample tool provided (see Figure 13.1) is a blend of technical and operational questions to establish a current baseline, but also to help show readiness and requirements for areas of the practice affected when adopting new technology. Because every practice is different, it is impossible to develop a tool that will provide an interpretation of your current situation based on your individual answers. Thus, this tool is a checklist for gathering information to help you communicate with vendors, contractors, staff members and anyone from the outside assisting you with the adoption of new technology.

Vendor Vetting Tools

This section of the chapter provides several sample tools to aid with vendor selection. These tools include the following:

■ Sample RFI
■ Sample RFP
■ Sample demo scripts
■ Sample score cards
■ Sample site visit checklist
■ Sample list of reference questions

Request for Information

Before diving deeply into vendor vetting, it is sometimes helpful to begin with gathering basic information about vendors. An RFI is usually a one- or two-page letter sent to vendors requesting information about their products and services. The RFI can be used to weed out vendors that may not meet your qualifications. You may want to state your minimal qualifications to not waste your time or the vendor's. For example, add a sentence that states you must be CCHIT-certified to respond to this RFI, which will eliminate any solution not eligible for stimulus funding.

READINESS ASSESSMENT CHECKLIST

General Information

1. Practice Name: _____

2. Other Owned Entities (Physician Network, Management Services Organization, Surgery Center, Clinic, etc.)

    ♦ _____

    ♦ _____

    ♦ _____

    ♦ _____

3. Taxpayer Identification Number? _____

    a. If multiple TIN, Identify purpose of each:

    TIN_____   Entity_____

    TIN_____   Entity_____

    TIN_____   Entity_____

4. What type of Practice? __Private __PHO __Rural Health __Community-Based __ Urgent Care

5. Please provide the practice specialty/specialties:

    ♦ _____

    ♦ _____

    ♦ _____

    ♦ _____

6. Total Number of Physicians? _____

    Total Number of Non-Physician Providers (NPPs), i.e., NP, PA, etc.? ___

7. Number of physical locations? _____ (List Below)

Physical Address	Number of Physicians	Number of NPP

Figure 13.1 Sample assessment checklist.

8. Other types of stand- alone facilities:

    a. Surgery Center (ASC) _____   Endoscopy Center_____

    b. Independent Diagnostic Testing Facility (IDTF)_____

    c. Independent Lab Service Center (Quest, LabCorp, etc.) _____

    d. Imaging Center_____

9. Identify other services provided in the practice:

    ____ **Radiology**

        __Flat Film __PACS __ Ultrasound __ MRI __CT __ Bone Density __Other

    ____ **Laboratory (On site)**

        __ Waived __Moderate __High Complexity __Phlebotomy Only

    ____ **Diagnostic Testing**

        __Endoscopy __Pulmonary Studies __Sleep Studies __Allergy Testing

        __Vascular Studies __Cardiac Studies __ Bronchoscopy __ Other_____

10. List all departments involved in patient care:

    ♦ _____

    ♦ _____

    ♦ _____

    ♦ _____

Office Accessibility

1. Do you use Personal computers, "Dumb" terminals or thin clients to access your systems with your environment? _____

2. Do all users have access to the Internet?   Yes   No

    a. If No, identify who does not have access: _____

3. If you have a remote locations/office(s), how are the offices connected?

    Dial up line ___Leased Line (56k)___ T1 Line ___ Internet Connection ___

Figure 13.1 (Continued)

4. Do you currently interface with other Lab(s) or Hospital(s) systems to send and receive tests?

___Yes   ___No

5. Lab(s) or Hospital(s) systems with which you presently interface or submit lab orders?

◆_____Bi-directional?_____

◆_____Bi-directional?_____

◆_____Bi-directional?_____

◆_____Bi-directional?_____

Do you currently participate in any regional arrangement to share electronic patient level clinical data through an electronic health information exchange?

___Yes, we participate and actively exchange data. The arrangement is with _____

___Yes, we participate but do not exchange data. The arrangement is with _____

___No, we do not participate in any regional arrangements to share patient information.

6. Does your system use HL7 messaging for data exchange between systems?   __Yes __No

7. What is your current bandwidth (please use "C") and bandwidth needs (Please use "N") to support EHR?

What is your current broadband access?	<5Mb/s	<15Mb/s	<25Mb/s	<50Mb/s	<75Mb/s	<75-100 Mb/s	<100Mb/s
What is your minimum upstream bandwidth for a broadband connection to support HIE?							
What is your minimum downstream bandwidth for a broadband connection to support HIE?							

Figure 13.1   (Continued)

What is your maximum upstream bandwidth requirement for a broadband connection to support HIE?							
What is your maximum downstream bandwidth requirement for a broadband connection to support HIE?							

Staffing/Expense Information - Related to HIS

1. How many FTEs are dedicated to registration/check in?

2. How many FTEs are dedicated to charge entry?

3. How many FTEs are dedicated to payment entry?

4. How many FTEs are dedicated to collections? self-pay and insurance?

5. How many FTEs are directly involved with the financial and administrative aspects of the practice including staff, management, IT, and clerical, but excluding physicians, clinicians, PAs, NPs, and Residents?

6. To whom do you presently transmit electronic claims?

7. Are charges entered at the time of service?

8. If not, when are charges entered?

9. Does your current system provide accurate encounter tracking or missing encounter form reports?

10. Does your current scheduling system allow each department to set their unique scheduling parameters, i.e., type, frequency, and duration?

11. Do you print statements in house or transmit them to a third party for preparation?

12. If you print statements in-house, how often do you print?

13. If you transmit to a 3rd party, how much do you pay per statement?

Figure 13.1   (Continued)

14. Do you make reminder calls for upcoming appointments?

15. If so, how many per month?

16. How many No-Shows do you have on average per day?

17. Do you charge for No-Shows?

18. Do you print/send recall letters or postcards?

19. Do you charge for medical records copying?

20. If so, how many admissions per month?

21. What is the average charge for a Patient visit/stay?

22. What is your annual Revenue?

23. What is your total Accounts Receivable Balance?

24. What is your total "self-pay" A/R Balance?

25. What is your total "self-pay" A/R Balance over 90 days?

26. What is your total "3rd Party Claims" outstanding Balance?

27. What is your total "3rd Party Claims" outstanding Balance over 90 days?

28. How are referral and patient letters generated? _____

29. How are test results communicated to the patients? _____

30. Do you have a tracking system for identifying outstanding results and appointments?
_____

31. How many FTEs are dedicated to pulling and filing Patient charts?

32. Annual compensation of chart management personnel (including benefits)?

33. How many paper medical records do you currently maintain onsite?

34. Do you use document storage facilities offsite?

35. Please indicate the method your Physicians use to document patient encounters.

36. How many FTEs are dedicated to transcription of records and letters?

37. Annual compensation of Transcription staff (including benefits)?

    a.   If you outsource transcription what is your annual transcription cost?

Figure 13.1 (Continued)

14. **Current EHR Information**

Which of the following HIT systems are installed in your practice(s)? Include vendor name, program version and CCHIT Certification Level.

	Vendor	Program Version	CCHIT Certification
Health Information System (HIS)			
Practice Management System			
Provider Credentialing Program			
Electronic Health Record (EHR)			
Managed Care Contract Management System			
Document Imaging/Scanning			
Insurance Eligibility & Verification			
Appointment Confirmation			
Lab/Test Result Messaging			
Online Patient Registration			
Online CPT-IV, ICD-9 and HCPCS Coding Resources			
Clinical Reference Systems (CRS)			
Electronic Prescription System			
Computerized Physician Order Entry (CPOE)			
Lab Information System (LIS)			
Radiology Information System (RIS)			
Picture Archiving and Communication System (PACS)			

EHR Goals

1. Please list the primary reasons you want to implement an EHR System?

_____

_____

_____

_____

Figure 13.1 **(Continued)**

2. How significant a barrier to implementation of an EHR system are the following:

	Major Barrier	Minor Barrier	Not a Barrier
Capital needed to purchase and implement			
Uncertain Return on Investment (ROI)			
Ongoing cost of maintaining EHR			
Resistance from physicians			
Resistance from other providers			
Resistance from staff			
Lack of ability to select, contract, and implement EHR			
Disruption in clinical care during implementation			
Lack of adequate IT staff or IT support			
Concerns about training providers and staff			
Concerns about Documentation & Coding			
Inappropriate disclosure of patient information			
Concerns about Medical Records (purging, scanning, uploading)			
Concerns about Upgrades and Lack of future support			

3. Which of the following models would be a preferred EHR data storage model for your practice?

__ Federated or distributed model (all EHR data stays at practice site)

__Hybrid model (some copies of patient data may reside outside the practice; practice has full EHR)

__Centralized model (EHR data are stored centrally with a vendor/data center)

Need more information (please explain)

_____

_____

Figure 13.1   (Continued)

4. Do you have dedicated HIT professionals in your practice? YES   NO (Indicate FTEs)

____ CIO/IT Director(s) ____ IT Application Administrators ____ IT Technicians

____ Data Warehouse Administrators/Analysts ____ Bio-Technicians
____ Informatics Nurses

_____ Other professionals trained in Informatics

5. Do you currently have a dedicated helpdesk system and staff for logging tickets and performing root cause analysis? YES   NO (If yes, how many FTEs_____)

Hardware / Software / and Projected Needs

Number of users who will use the system for access to patient information, scheduling, charge entry, payment entry, reporting and collections:

Number of users who will access the EHR System for access to patient records:

          Doctors ____ NP/PA _____Nurses _____Admin/Support Staff _____

Number of PCs installed at the nurse's stations: _____

Number of PCs installed in other clinical areas: _____

          Identify the other clinical areas:_____

Number of PCs installed at the front desk: _____

Number of PCs installed for the billing staff: _____

Number of PCs installed in other clerical areas: _____

          Identify the other clerical areas:_____

Total number of PCs in the practice (existing PCs): _____

Total laser printers for printing face sheets, encounter forms, HCFAs, reports, etc.: _____

Total other printers for printing face sheets, encounter forms, HCFAs, reports, etc.: _____

Number of insurance card scanners: _____

Number of Multi-purpose Copiers in the practice: _____

Location(s) of copiers: _____

Technical Assessment of Existing IT infrastructure:

1. Type of Server Presently installed (include how peripherals and terminals are connected):

_____

Figure 13.1   (Continued)

2. What type of workstations do you have deployed? _____

   a. Type of terminals installed/number of units? _____

   b. Type of personal computers (PCs) installed / Number of Units?

_____

   c. Type of Thin Clients/Number of units? _____

3. Version of operating system? _____

   a. On the servers? _____

   b. On the workstations?_____

4. Applications installed? _____

5. Type of hub or switch installed?_____

6. Number of ports available? _____

7. Does the site currently have access to the Internet? Who is the provider? Copy of statement: _____

8. Check to see if there is adequate power supply at the Dmarc Location and at PC location

_____

9. Printers and types _____

   Type of cabling installed?_____

10. Who is currently supporting your infrastructure? _____

11. How do you back-up your current system? _____

12. Describe your disaster recovery/business continuity plan?

_____

_____

As stated above, this assessment tool is only intended to gather information for areas of operations or technical requirements affected from adopting new technology. As each practice is different, the practice should customize this tool accordingly.

Figure 13.1 (Continued)

Here is a sample RFI:

Sample RFI

[Date]

Dear [Vendor _Company Name] _____

This request for information (RFI) is for information only. It is not a solicitation for bids or an offer of a contract. Responses will not bind the vendor contractually or financially, or in any other way, but will provide _ [name of practice/organization] _____with information and comparisons if the practice does go forward with a request for proposals (RFP). It is the intention of the practice to generate an RFP based on information received from this RFI.

Responders are requested to:

1. Supply a brief corporate overview.
2. Send marketing brochures, demo disk and other information to educate us on your products and services.
3. Not provide unsolicited information over the telephone at this time.
4. Number of systems installed in the state of [state name] _____.
5. Number of systems installed in practices over [the number of] ____ providers.
6. Number of systems installed in [state specialty] _____

Please submit your responses to [name] ___ at the address below.
Responses must be received by [date] __
Questions and comments should be directed to [name] _____

Request for Proposal

An RFP is a comprehensive document describing the desired functional requirements for vendors to provide and deliver. Each vendor will complete the same RFP, allowing you the opportunity to contract and compare vendors based on their ability to meet your functionality requirements. The RFP should be written clearly and concisely so that the vendors' response teams do not have to guess your meaning. Use simple terms and direct questions (e.g., use vs utilize) – your goal is to be clear, so that you get precise responses.

Request for Proposal (RFP) sample documents are available for HIMSS members at https://www.himss.org/rfp-sample-documents-0. The web page explains the samples as follows:

These Request for Proposal (RFP) sample documents are provided as tools for use by a healthcare organization and other healthcare providers in developing its own RFP. They provide a structured approach for the various criteria that may be relevant to the organization's own RFP process, including general information and experience; technical information regarding architecture; applications; and services. The documents provide sample requirements and narrative questions relevant to the section. In addition, there are sample methodologies for evaluating vendor responses received.

These documents are designed to be a starting point for your RFP; the questions and requirements are meant to be illustrative, not exhaustive. Some items may apply to an organization's particular situation and others may not. It is expected that each organization will make changes specific to its procurement, including changing, adding, or deleting items to tailor the RFP for its specific use. It is recommended that any organization using these documents ensure they involve experts in the functional areas to ensure that detailed business requirements are gathered.

To create your RFP, we suggest using all of the documents from Section I and selecting documents from Section II as appropriate to your organization's need. Section III includes score sheets to be tailored for use during the vendor selection process.

Search the HIMSS Online Buyer's guide by category for potential vendors to send your completed RFP.

Sample Demo Script

Every vendor comes prepared to show you "THEIR" version of the demo. They will also use a demo script, built in advance and designed to be perfect. Using a demo script developed exclusively for the practice is a great tool to force vendors to demonstrate the exact same functionality to determine how their efficiencies compare. Individually, it will also show the vendor's ability to be flexible on the fly. For example, the first vendor may struggle to get through the demo scripts because their system is not complete, while a more qualified vendor can breeze through it because their system is more comprehensive. Without a demo script, you will only see what the vendor wants to show you, and you can guarantee it will be something they pre-built to make their system look good.

VENDOR DEMO				
General Visit, health maintenance alerts, lab request, e-script, Coding				

Patient name	Earnie Baker		ESTABLISHED PATIENT	
Date of Service	today			
Demographics	Male, non-smoker			
	(address, etc. - whatever you want)			
Medical history	Medical History: arthritis, hypertension. Medication List: Zocor 40mg QD, Hydrochlorothiazide 50mg QD, Celebrex 200mg QD, Allergic to penicillin: Prior BP 130/80, Pulse 85, Weight 160, Height 69"			
CHIEF COMPLAINT	Frequent urination and burning			

Venue / Stage of Process	User		Interaction with system	Comments
Ambulatory Clinic				
Patient Care	RN or MA	1	RN/MA asks initial assessment questions. Pt states that he has noticed frequent urination for past 3 weeks. In past 5 days, there is some burning. (office lab processing UA & sending specimen for culture) No blood. Vital signs, Wt 167, BP 152/94, Pulse 80.	
	RN or MA		During review, nurse sees health maintenance alert that patient is past due for PSA. She advises patient.	
Patient Care	Doctor-Exam	2	On examination - Well developed, well nourished, slight tenderness in abdomen, no edema of legs or feet.	Demo system's charting methodology, mention lab interfaces
	Doctor-Assessment/ Plan	3	1. Probable UTI, write script for ampicillin; changed script to Cipro 2. Order urine culture	System presents drug allergy alert
		4	Diagnosis: Urinary Tract Infection, suspected	
E&M	Doctor-reviews coding	5	Review E&M coding, automatic coding, etc., how EMR can help prevent missed charges, etc.	

Sample Vendor Demo Scorecard

An essential tool for vetting vendors is a demo scorecard. Vendor demos may take place over several weeks, each lasting three to four hours. The scorecard helps you keep track of your likes and dislikes as each vendor presents. Without a scorecard it can be easy to forget or confuse notable features about each vendor. The scorecard is also a way to help your selection committee build a consensus towards a preferred vendor based on defined objectives and based on overall performance. Without this tool, the committee can stall by debating options and sometimes make poor decisions, especially when there is someone who can easily influence opinion without a justification based on what is best for the practice.

Here is a sample vendor scorecard:

Vendor Presentation Scorecard

Rating Scale

1: Poor	2: Below Average	3: Adequate	4: Good	5: Excellent

Please rate the vendor's presentations based on the above rating scale.

Characteristics and Qualities	Vendor 1	Vendor 2
Your impression based on their corporate overview		
Your impression based on their accomplishments		
Your impression of the appearance of the application (design, workflow)		
Will support/improve your job		
Ease of use (easy to understand the workflow)		
Ability to improve reimbursement		
Layout of the screen, navigation, accessibility of information		
Ease of inner office communication (i.e., doctor–nurse/ nurse–receptionist…)		
Ease of data entry		
Overall workflow efficiency		
Ability to deliver/improve the quality of care		
Overall impression of the application		
Total		

Comments

Vendor 1 Positives

_____

_____

Vendor 1 Negatives

_____

_____

Vendor 2 Positives

Vendor 2 Negatives

_____

_____

Sample Site Visit Checklist

Another great tool for conducting vendor site visits is using a checklist. This will help you stay consistent in capturing information and allow you to later make an apples-to-apples comparison.

Here is a sample form for conducting a vendor site visit:

Representing:	☐ Information technology ☐ Physicians ☐ Ancillaries ☐Patient care/management ☐ Registration
With whom did you meet: Contact: Name: _____ Phone: _____ E-mail: _____ Dept: _____	
Checklist: ☐ Functionality review: ☐ User training: How much? Was it enough? ☐ Implementation timeline: What came up and when? ☐ How much was customized by the vendor or the hospital? Who did the customization, i.e., end-users, IS? ☐ Did they get what they thought they would get?	

Overall:
1. How similar was the software to what was demonstrated?
2. How broadly was the system being used?
3. What were the lessons learned?
4. What were the surprises?
5. What were the goals of the facility and were these achieved?
6. How much scheduled / unscheduled downtime?
7. How does this system help communication between departments?
8. How does this system assist with following policies and procedures?

Department Functionality:
☐ What specific department functionality is being used?
☐ What is still done manually and why?
☐ What reports are you receiving?
☐ What works well? What works poorly?
☐ What are you planning to change?
☐ Was the vendor's staff helpful for the department during implementation?
☐ How flexible are screens, forms and reports?
☐ How responsive is the system (speed)?
☐ How much help is available online?
☐ After a downtime what information must be re-entered into the system?
☐ Has the system made your job easier?

List of Reference Questions

One of the last and most important steps to make a good vendor decision is to conduct reference checks. Here is a list of questions to consider when conducting reference calls:

- What were the top five reasons for selecting the software?
- How did the software perform vs expectations?
- What was the quality of vendor training?
- What was the quality of the implementation team?
- Did the vendor meet deadlines?
- Did the vendor stay on budget?
- What was the attitude of vendor's staff (friendly, adversarial, etc.)?
- How did the vendor deal with problems during implementation?
- How were the problems resolved?
- Where there any system defects; if so, how were they corrected?
- What are the top five major benefits of the software?

- What are the top five major limitations of the software? Did the vendor respond promptly to issues or concerns?
- Were there any hidden or unexpected costs?
- How were interfaces handled?
- Did you do a data conversion? Was it successful?
- How did the vendor respond to difficulties?
- What other vendors did you consider, and why did you not select them?
- If you had to do it over again, would you still choose the same vendor?

Return on Investment (ROI) Tool

An ROI is common tool used to measure the financial benefits/gains of adopting an EHR. When completing an ROI before implementing the EHR, there will have to be assumptions made in order to use this tool. It is recommended that you use conservative assumptions to avoid misrepresenting the financial benefits and to consider both hard and soft costs. For example, it is easy to estimate the cost of the software because the vendor will provide you with a quote but estimating the cost of lost physician productivity is a bit more challenging. Some productivity loss will occur; thus, it is best to predict the worst to avoid setting unrealistic expectations. It is common to see a 20 to 30% reduction in physician productivity over the first 4 to 6 weeks, so budget accordingly. Also, make sure to capture miscellaneous expenses, such as cabling, travel expenses and extra equipment. You may also want to add about 10% costs for unexpected circumstances.

Here is a sample ROI Tool:

Practice Name: xxxx	Year	Year		
	Before EMR Implementation	*After EMR Implementation*	*Difference*	*Percent Difference*
Number of FTE – providers	5	5	0	0.00%
Number of FTE mid-levels	1	1	0	0.00%
Total providers	6	6	0	0.00%

(Continued)

Practice Name: xxxx	Year	Year		
	Before EMR Implementation	*After EMR Implementation*	*Difference*	*Percent Difference*
Number of admin staff	12	10	(2)	−16.67%
Number of clinical staff	6	6	0	0.00%
Total annual charges	$6,000,000.00	$7,440,000.00	$1,440,000.00	24.00%
Total charges per month	$500,000.00	$620,000.00	$120,000.00	24.00%
Charges per provider per month	$83,333.33	$103,333.33	$20,000.00	24.00%
Charges per provider per day (21 business days per month)	$3,968.25	$4,920.63	$952.38	24.00%
Total patient visits per month (doctors)	2500	2550	50	2.00%
Patient visits per provider per month	417	425	8	2.00%
Patient visits per provider per day (21 business days per month)	20	20	0	2.00%
Current insurance aging	$400,000.00	$380,000.00	$ (20,000.00)	−5.00%

(*Continued*)

Practice Name: xxxx	Year	Year		
	Before EMR Implementation	*After EMR Implementation*	*Difference*	*Percent Difference*
30 to 60 insurance aging	$150,000.00	$140,000.00	**$(10,000.00)**	**–6.67%**
60 to 90 insurance aging	$185,000.00	$80,000.00	**$(105,000.00)**	**–56.76%**
90 to 120 insurance aging	$35,000.00	$50,000.00	**$(5,000.00)**	**–9.09%**
120 plus insurance aging	$20,000.00			
Total insurance aging	*$790,000.00*	*$650,000.00*	*$(140,000.00)*	*–17.72%*
Current patient aging	$40,000.00	$38,000.00	**$(2,000.00)**	**–5.00%**
30 to 60 patient aging	$25,000.00	$23,000.00	**$(2,000.00)**	**–8.00%**
60 to 90 patient aging	$15,000.00	$10,000.00	**$(5,000.00)**	**–33.33%**
90 to 120 patient aging	$12,000.00	$26,000.00	**$(1,000.00)**	**–3.70%**
120 plus patient aging	$15,000.00			
Total patient aging	*$107,000.00*	*$97,000.00*	*$(10,000.00)*	*–9.35%*
Total accounts receivable	*$897,000.00*	*$747,000.00*	*$(150,000.00)*	*–16.72%*
Accounts receivable per provider	*$149,500.00*	*$124,500.00*	*$(25,000.00)*	*–16.72%*
How many new patients do you see daily?	16			

(*Continued*)

Practice Name: xxxx	Year	Year		
	Before EMR Implementation	*After EMR Implementation*	*Difference*	*Percent Difference*
Business days per year (12 × 21)	252			
Total new patients	4,032			
Chart cost ($3 per new paper chart)	**$12,096.00**	Savings		
Cost savings for not purchasing additional chart rack after EMR implementation	x	Savings		
What were/are your annual transcription costs?	$61,000.00	$5,000.00	**$(56,000.00)**	**−91.80%**
Transcription cost per provider (annual)	**$10,166.67**	**$833.33**	**$(9,333.33)**	**−91.80%**
Transcription cost per provider (monthly)	**$847.22**	**$69.44**	**$(777.78)**	**−91.80%**

HIPAA Security Checklist

	Yes	No
Have you completed an annual risk assessment of the potential risks and vulnerabilities related to the confidentiality, integrity and availability of personal health information?		

(*Continued*)

	Yes	No
Have you created an inventory of all computers, laptops, mobile devices, printers and other equipment used by your organization?		
Have you identified where sensitive data are stored? Have you identified who has access to these data?		
Do you have all written policies and procedures for all standards and implementation specifications in the HIPAA security rule?		
Have you identified a security officer within your organization?		
Do you have a risk management plan?		
Do you change your passwords frequently, and are your passwords complex?		
Do you regularly audit and disable outdated employee accounts?		
Do you have an e-mail security filtering system (spam filtering)?		
Are all records backed up off-site (cloud, data center, etc.)?		
Has a due diligence review been conducted on your organizations service providers and other third-party vendors to ensure they have documented safeguards in place against breaches?		
Do you have written documentation (certificate, sign off sheet, etc.) of HIPAA security training for employees, including ongoing security awareness training that covers your practice's HIPAA security policies?		
Do you limit and log access to the physical locations or rooms that contain servers or network devices (i.e., server room)?		
Do you have a commercial-grade firewall(s) in place?		
Do workstations automatically lock the screen and require logging back in after a specific time of inactivity?		
Do you have a signed business associates agreement (BAA) as revised by the 2013 HIPAA Omnibus Rule for all vendors who may access, store or transmit PHI? (IT vendors, printer companies, third-party vendors, online data storing systems, etc.)		
Have you performed a quarterly vulnerability scan/assessment on your network?		
Do you have a way to encrypt e-mail messages that may contain PHI?		
Do you have documentation that all workstations, servers and mobile devices that contain PHI are encrypted?		

(Continued)

	Yes	No
Are your Microsoft, Adobe and Java products up to date?		
Does your organization use anti-virus software on all devices accessing the organization's network (this also includes mobile devices)?		
Are anti-virus updates run on a regular and continuous basis?		
Do you have a plan and procedure in place to notify your clients immediately in the case of a security breach or incident?		
Do you have cybersecurity insurance that will protect your business?		
Do you have a process in place for retrieving backed-up data and archived copies of information?		
Have you created a business continuity/disaster recovery plan to implement in the event of a cybersecurity event?		

1: Poor	2: Below Average	3: Adequate	4: Good	5: Excellent	N/A

Please rate the vendor's software applications based on the above rating scale.

Practice Management System (PM)			
Characteristics and Features	*Vendor 1*	*Vendor 2*	*Vendor 3*
Scheduling features			
Patient check-in/check-out features			
Patient registration features			
Ease of collecting uniform data system (UDS) information at registration			
Billing function			
Sliding fee scales			
Accounts receivable			
Layout of the screens, navigation, accessibility of information			

(Continued)

Practice Management System (PM)			
Characteristics and Features	*Vendor 1*	*Vendor 2*	*Vendor 3*
Ease of data entry			
Easy to understand the workflow			
Will this PM system support/improve your job?			
Does vendor offer patient portal for scheduling and registration?			
Reports – do the standard ones meet your needs?			
Ability to print multilingual statements and doctor's orders?			
Ease of producing a UDS report			
Overall impression of the application			
Total points			

Electronic Medical Record (EMR)			
Characteristics and Features	*Vendor 1*	*Vendor 2*	*Vendor 3*
Layout of the screens, navigation, accessibility of information			
Workflow and use of system intuitive to the clinicians			
Ease of data entry			
Ease of inner-office communication			
Ease of documenting the "Oh-by-the-ways"			
Drug-to-drug, drug-to-allergy reaction function?			
Rx script feature – formularies preferred and available?			
Management of sample medications			
Lab feature – ability to interface incoming results			

(*Continued*)

Electronic Medical Record (EMR)			
Characteristics and Features	*Vendor 1*	*Vendor 2*	*Vendor 3*
Charting feature is easy to use			
Handwriting recognition?			
Templates to guide and support developmental exams			
Vaccine management			
Customization of templates and screens meets your needs, and ease of customization			
Functionality for receiving/tracking diagnostic studies			
Function for receiving/tracking referrals meets needs?			
Reporting			
Does the patient portal support patient entry of medical history information?			
Overall impression of the application?			
Total points			

Index

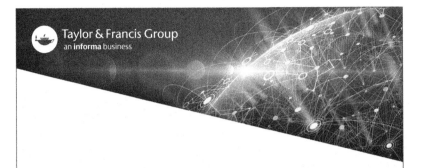